GOING GOING GONE

The Story of Britain's Vanishing
Natural History

Nicholas Schoon

For each copy of this book sold, £1 of the purchase price will go to WWF-UK's Site
Safeguard Fund. This exists to finance legal actions aimed at protecting threatened
wildlife sites in Britain and to provide grants for other conservation organisations to
purchase endangered habitats.

The WWF-UK (World Wide Fund for Nature) was founded in 1961
and is committed to saving threatened wildlife species and habitats. It
researches, lobbies governments, raises funds and sets up its own
conservation projects worldwide. WWF-UK aims to build a future
in which people live in harmony with nature.

© Bookman Projects Ltd and Nicholas Schoon 1996
Design and typesetting by Kerry Counsell & Diane Wilkinson.
Scanning and Image Quality: John Symonds
Printed in the UK by SGC Printing on Envirocote.

ISBN 1 898718 39 3

CONTENTS

ACKNOWLEDGEMENTS

I was helped by many people and organisations in the course of researching and writing this book and the series of articles which preceded it. Particularly helpful were: Charles Arther, Keith Corbett, Charles Cuthbert, Gordon Dixon, Mike Edwards, Clare Garner, Tony Gent, Glyn Griffiths, Chris Harbard and the RSPB, Brian Harris, the hard pressed but efficient picture desk of the Independent, Nick Kent, Peter Lambley, Tom Langton, Chris Newbold, Phil Page, Robin Pellew, the staff of Plantlife, Gary Roberts, Chris Tydeman, the Vincent Wildlife Trust, Paul Waring, Martin Willing, Charles Wilson, Robert Wolton and Ros Wynne-Jones.

The staff of English Heritage, Scottish Natural Heritage and the Environment Agency dug up a treasure trove of photographs and supplied much useful information.

I am also very grateful to Michael Johnson, my brother-in-law, for the loan of the laptop computer on which much of this was written. Most thanks of all to my wife Julie and my children, who put up with me writing this book during a school summer holidays which included two weeks when we were away from home together.

Foreword

Most of us have become accustomed to the idea that mankind is wiping out species and habitats, and that our behaviour in rainforests, undersea and throughout crowded foreign habitats is steadily destroying the biodiversity and richness of Earth. Most of us are intermittently worried about it, aware of campaigns on Brazilian logging, Asian tigers or Antarctic whales. This knowledge, this anxiety, are part of what it means to be an alert human in the late 1990s. But there are two general problems, or failures, in how many of us think about the destruction of nature. First, we tend to regard it as an exotic threat, something driven by the poverty of farmers or the greed of multinationals, or human ignorance, overseas. Too few of us are fully aware of the destruction of species and the threat to many more right here in Britain. And second, we tend to be passive and even despairing about mankind's blundering trail of destruction; it is something so big, so intimately connected to the global industrial economy and the earth's fast-rising human population, as to be insoluble. With a shiver of guilt, but little optimism, we put our coins in green plastic collecting-boxes decorated with elephants or whales: we don't really expect the small platoons of campaigners to stop the march of history.

"Going, Going, Gone", Nicholas Schoon's superb survey of the state of nature conservation, published with World Wide Fund for Nature, derives from his award-winning reporting for the Independent. It helps correct both these serious failings. He focuses on the British Isles and provides an authoritive survey of the species and habitats under threat in what he calls "Grey Britain". Tigers are romantic; but there are serious biodiversity challenges under our noses too. Second, by detailing how leading conservation groups, working with the Government, are helping rescue endangered species and habitats, it is a timely and useful corrective for those with an innate tendency to shrug. This is an issue that affects the whole meaning and texture of these islands, as well as being a global challenge. It is not a hopeless cause, nor a dry one. Here is a book which, besides being packed with information, can serve as a manifesto for the millions of us who want to help.

Andrew Marr, Editor, The Independent.

Preface

We are today faced with a wave of mass extinctions. Based on the latest satellite imagery of the loss of forests and other habitats, the best estimate for the rate of species extinctions is about 3% per decade. This may not sound particularly serious, but when translated into a figure in excess of a quarter of a million species each year, it becomes very alarming indeed. However, the great majority of these species will be microscopic beetles in the canopy of tropical trees or minute soil mites in the forest floor litter.

Over the last four hundred years some 300 species of vertebrates are known to have gone extinct, and of these only a tiny handful are the sorts of high mammals that people get worked up about - like the quagga and bluebuck of South Africa, the Tasmanian wolf and the Caribbean monk seal. We are very good at saving species on the point of extinction through emergency measures like captive breeding or habitat manipulation, but whilst we are willing to do this for the Jarvan rhino or Californian condor, what about the Mexican totoaba (it's a sort of fish) or the St Helena giant earwig?

Closer to home, the United Kingdom may not be endowed with the diversity of species of the tropics, but with its extensive coastline and range of landscapes from river meadows to mountain tops, it does have a highly varied and mixed diversity of habitats. The UK has about 1,400 species of vascular plants, about 48 species of mammals, and some 210 species of breeding birds. On an area basis, this makes us one of the more species rich of the Northern European countries.

Since 1900, more than 100 species have become extinct in the UK, including such peculiarities as the greater mouse-eared bat, the burbot, and the Essex emerald moth. And many more species are rapidly declining. The backbone of the UK conservation effort is the network of some 6,000 designated Sites of Special Scientific Interest. Current estimates reckon that around 5% of these sites, some 300, are damaged or partly destroyed each year. Once common farmland birds like the song thrush, grey partridge and corn bunting are now becoming rarer, and when did you last hear a skylark or nightingale? Britain is losing its biological diversity just as certainly as Brazil, Madagascar or Indonesia - it is happening here at home and the situation is urgent.

So what is to be done to reverse this decline? This is the main theme of this book -action plans for the recovery and restoration of our species and habitats. Under the auspices of the Department of Environment, a programme is now being put into place for the conservation of some 400 of the most threatened species and 38 of the key habitats throughout the UK. For the first time, we now have a fully costed programme, including targets against which we can monitor success, for the recovery of British wildlife. We now need to get on and do it.

As always, the problem is money. Once the programme is fully running, it will require some £50 million per annum. This is the cost of saving our natural inheritance. In absolute terms it may seem a lot, but compared to the billions of pounds paid every year to subsidise British agriculture, which is probably the main threat to so much of our wildlife, it's peanuts. Shifting just 5% from destroying our wildlife to saving it would do the trick. £50 million seems a very modest budget to save our wildlife, yet it is regarded as an unacceptable burden on the public purse.

The only way to resolve this is through you, the reader. What are your priorities for public spending? If, like me, you believe there is a moral duty on any government in power to safeguard our inheritance, then let your voice be heard - express your opinions to your local MP or the Prime Minister, or even a conservation organisation like WWF! Hundreds of millions are spent on protecting our cultural heritage, so why not our natural inheritance as well?

It is worth the effort - otters are now re-colonising their previous haunts, sea eagles once again fly over the cliffs of Western Scotland, ospreys and red kites are again becoming common in our wilder countryside, and even the large blue butterfly is back again on the grasslands of south west England. We can reverse the decline if we have the determination and commitment to do so. And you can make the difference, for remember, extinction is for ever.

Robin Pellew, Director, WWF-UK

INTRODUCTION

Among the world's tens of thousands of butterfly species there is a pretty blue one which has a particularly violent and disgusting youth. This is its life cycle. The large blue (which, despite it name, is a little smaller than the red admirals and cabbage whites fluttering around your garden) places its eggs on the flower buds of thyme plants early in July. The tiny caterpillars hatch out and feed on the flowers and leaves for three weeks, then drop to the ground. There a species of red ant, *Myrmica sabuleti*, is attracted by sweet, sticky excretions from the caterpillar's hairy body. After a while the ant picks up the larva in its jaws and hefts it into the nest it shares with hundreds of its fellows. It does so because it is programmed to collect and bring home scattered ant grubs and it mistakes the butterfly's baby as one - the caterpillar is of just the right size, texture and hairiness.

Big mistake. The caterpillar has mandibles which are large, sharp and powerful. It uses these formidable jaws to burst open the tender ant grubs crowded underground then devours the resulting mess of body fluids and soft skin. Over the next few months it eats hundreds of the grubs, growing fat and ugly and sometimes wiping out the ant colony in the process, before becoming a bloated chrysalis. Then, next summer, the adult butterfly emerges from the devastated nest. It lives and flies for only about six days during which it mates, the eggs are produced and the cycle recommences.

You would think such a weird and unsettling wildlife story comes from deep in a tropical rain forest, but the butterfly lives here in Britain. The large blue's tale illustrates most of the themes in this book. It hints at life on earth's endless strangeness, intricacy and ingenuity and the unnerving combination of great beauty and utter ruthlessness which underlie our fascination with nature. Then there is the fact that this particular species actually became extinct in Britain in 1979 after a century of steady decline. That was due to the waning of its very particular type of habitat which, in turn, was caused by human actions or, rather, inactions. But now the large blue is back, thanks to further human intervention.

Dr Jeremy Thomas, of the Government's Institute of Terrestrial Ecology, studied the insect and its exploitation of the ant closely, trying to find out why previous conservation attempts had failed. He discovered its precise requirements at about the same time as it finally disappeared from Britain. More than anything else, the large blue needs thyme plants and the one particular species of red ant. And the ant itself needs warmth, which means it has to live among short-grazed grass less than two inches tall on south facing slopes. Only then can enough sunshine reach down to the ground where it scurries around. The reason why this habitat existed in Britain was because farmers have grazed their sheep and cattle on such slopes for centuries. But the ant's populations became fewer and fewer, more and more scattered, either because this habitat was more intensively farmed - ploughed, crop-planted, sprayed with fertilisers and pesticides - or because the rough grazing was abandoned in favour of intensive grass growing on flatter slopes. When the cattle and sheep were removed the downland grass grew tall, scrub invaded and the increased shading lowered ground level temperatures and wiped out the ant. Myxomatosis speeded up the process, by killing off the rabbits which helped to keep the grass short. The ant never became extinct in Britain but the large blue did, because to survive it needed big ant populations with a high density of nests.

This understanding paved the way for the large blue's successful reintroduction in Britain. The conditions both it and the ant insist on are maintained at five carefully chosen and still secret sites in the the last 40 years as in the previous 400. But the four years between 1992 and 1996 will, hopefully, come to be seen as a turning point.

Why this optimism? Because in 1992 at the UN Earth Summit in Rio de Janeiro John Major was among more than 150 prime ministers and presidents who signed the Biodiversity Convention, an international treaty aimed at conserving

■ The Large Blue

Photography: J. Thomas/WWF

Cotswolds and coastal river valleys in Devon and Cornwall. Starting with large blue caterpillars imported from Sweden, butterfly colonies have been established at all five. Conservationists are now planning to reintroduce the species to a further five locations where the ant is still found. Managing the habitat for the large blue's benefit has brought further wildlife benefits; it suits other rare or declining creatures such as the woodlark and some fritillary butterflies.

Each year we learn more about the diversity of wildlife which lives in Britain, about its precise requirements and the threats we pose to it. We now know that as much or more damage has been done in the world's unimaginably huge diversity of living things. Biodiversity is a new and still awkward bit of jargon which is used to describe this richness - if you find it rather nerdish just substitute that fine, old-fashioned word 'nature' instead*. By 1996 the UK government had reached an agreement with almost all of the major nature conservation organisations in Britain on a framework for delivering Britain's treaty commitment as far as our own diminished wildlife is concerned. This book is about that wildlife and that agreement, but it begins by explaining why the world has such breathtaking biodiversity, how it has come to be endangered on every continent and in every ocean and what its prospects are.

* Scientists use biodiversity to refer not just to the richness of species but also to the diversity of habitats and to the genetic variation found within species

Chapter One

THE ORIGIN OF THE SPECIES

Life awes us for all sorts of reasons, but its sheer variety and the way in which it gets almost everywhere impress us most of all. You find it in the driest and hottest deserts and in the coldest seas, from mountain peaks down to the floor of the deepest oceans and in caves and aquifers which have had neither sunlight nor fresh air for millions of years. Following the discovery of what seem to be fossil microbes on a meteorite we now have reason to believe life got going on Mars. 'Nature abhors a vacuum,' the saying goes, but the truth is that nature adores a vacuum. It flings itself at every empty bit of space, thrilled at the challenge, and soon has it covered.

In taking over the earth's surface over the past four billion years life has assumed an incredible variety of forms. Most of these are invisibly small but there are trees the height of a modest skyscraper and coral reefs as long as countries. There are viruses so simple you could write their entire genetic code - the molecular instructions for building and operating them - on one small piece of paper, and then there are living things as complex as us.

Just south of Peterborough, on the utterly flat Cambridgeshire fenlands, life is busy showing off these qualities. Here is a huge pit covering more than one hundred hectares where giant excavators scoop out the stiff, almost dry Oxfordshire clay to a depth of ten metres. They work their way back and forth along one long, straight edge of Orton pit gradually pushing this side, the clayface, forward into undisturbed land. As they advance the cranes leave a strange and initially desolate landscape behind them. The poorer quality clay and the overlying soil which

cannot be used in the nearby brickmaking kilns are discarded into steep, conical hillocks on the floor of the pit. These miniature spoil heaps, each about six metres high, extend backwards in parallel lines to the opposite side of the pit more than half a mile away, which is where the work of extracting the clay began 40 years ago. Water collects in shallow pools between these rows of hillocks.

To us the land appears as a useless mess. The water, the steep slopes and bogginess of the sticky clay make the ground extremely difficult to cross. It costs Hanson, the conglomerate which owns it, approaching £250,000 a hectare to sort, resculpt and drain the land to the point where something commercially useful can be done with it - which, in this case, happens to be building a large chunk of a £500m township with homes for 13,000 people there.

But wildlife, which struggles amid the pesticides, herbicides and heavy fertiliser use on the big, intensively farmed cereal fields all around Peterborough, is wildly enthusiastic about the pit and has set up home there. At the clayface the first line of spoil hillocks is quite bare, but a few yards back where the ground has lain undisturbed for a year or more plants have established themselves. At first the vegetation consists of just two species adapted to this poor and difficult ground, colts foot and bristly ox-tongue. As you move further back into the older parts of the pit the vegetation becomes more varied - both open and dense scrub made of shrubs such as elder, the odd birch tree, grasses. More than 40 species of flowering plants and trees have colonised the ground, and almost 40 have been recorded growing in the pools. Fifteen species of dragonfly and damselfly flit over the pools, hunting for the dozens of species of insect which now live in the pit. A pair of hobbies, a rare bird of prey, have been hunting there for themselves and their young; they are agile and swift enough to catch the dragonflies, birds of prey of the insect world. Brown hares, which have been particularly hard hit by modern farming, have arrived and so have the foxes which hunt them. The species which seems to have gained the most from Orton Pit is the great crested newt, a rare and endangered amphibian. It mates and leaves its eggs in the pools in spring, then roams the vegetation on the spoil heaps gobbling up insects and worms (and the occasional smooth newt, a smaller species also found there). The

So here, in one patch of fresh habitat, is a healthy variety of native plant and animal species. Some of the Orton colonists are fairly rare across Britain, endangered by our unwitting refusal to share the land we use for farming, homes, roads and workplaces with other life forms. And on the floor of the pit lies evidence of the colossal variety and abundance of life stretching back into an incomprehensibly distant past. You cannot walk more than a few yards inside it without finding fossils from the marine species which teemed here 150 million years ago, when the clay was the bed of long gone sea. Mostly these are the remains of ammonites and belemnites, both squid-like molluscs, but if you are lucky you might find a bone from a plesiosaur, the 'Loch Ness monster' reptile which hunt-

■ Great crested newts at Orton Pit, with brick kiln chimneys in the background. Photography: Brian Harris

great crested has built up a population of tens of thousands at Orton; it is thought to be its largest colony in Europe.

ed fish in Jurassic seas, or even a fragment of a dinosaur's skeleton washed down from the coast.

Sand lizard - one of Britain's few reptile species.

Photography: Hugh Clark/WWF

The reason why this particular clay has been used to make billions of bricks is because it is chock-full of the remains of living things; full enough to fire the clay from the combustion of the mortal remains within. Dead plants and animals, the bulk of them of only microscopic size, sank to the bottom of the long gone Jurassic sea along with sediment from eroding rocks. As the layers accumulated and the pressure built up the chemistry of this organic matter changed. Today the remains of life are a kind of sulphurous, oily fuel mixed in with the clay minerals. Once the initial temperature of the raw clay is raised high enough by an outside heat source it self-combusts, turning the soft bricks rock hard.

Behind this variety and pervasiveness of life stretching back over the aeons is speciation, the formation of new species. This process is one of the absolute essentials of evolution. When it happens a new, slightly altered kind of plant or animal splits off from a founder species. This new species is adapted to an environment which is a little different from that experienced by the founder and the genes which specify how it is built and how it operates are slightly different too. It no longer breeds with the founder. Later, another new species can split off from this second species, or the founder species can split again. As well as giving birth to numerous descendent species in these ways the founder can also die - indeed, most species have become extinct within a dozen million years of their formation. Sometimes an entire lineage of species, the founder and all of those descended from it, become extinct; it has proved to be an evolutionary dead end. But the big picture is of the number of species gradually building up throughout the earth's history, producing ever more varied, widespread and complex plants and animals.

Consider the conquest of the land by the vertebrates, that huge group of animals with backbones which embraces all fish, amphibians, reptiles, birds and mammals. About 350 million years ago some fish became adapted to spend part of their time on land. We can imagine several good reasons why. They might have lived in freshwater pools which shrank or disappeared altogether during dry seasons, so that their chances of survival were greatly increased if they could crawl to other larger pools nearby. Perhaps they started spending time ashore to exploit the rich new food sources there; the plants and insects which had already evolved to colonise the land millions of years before them. Possibly several fish species in different parts of the world adapted to spending some of their lives on land, with natural selection altering their genes so that they could respire out

one species of fish out of water which founded the 25,000 different species of amphibians, reptiles, birds and mammals estimated to exist today. The original fish has itself been extinct for hundreds of millions of years (although a distant relative, the coelacanth, swims in the deep sea off Madagascar and the Comoro Islands).

Speciation leads to great evolutionary breakthroughs and the founding of triumphant dynasties. It was one new species of fish which gave rise to the first amphibians. Then it was one new species among the early amphibia which gave rise to the first reptiles. And, among the tens

■ Porpoises off the Scottish coast -
A mammal which has returned to the sea.

Photography: Dr Ben Wilson/University of Aberdeen

of water and use fins and tails to move across dry ground. But the fossil record and the anatomy of all the land vertebrates alive today indicate that it was just

of thousands of reptile species descending from this first over tens of millions of years, it was just one which founded all the mammals and another which founded all the birds. Speciation is behind all the great inventions of life, such as powered flight (developed separately by birds, insects, mammals and reptiles) and the feeding and sheltering of developing embryos inside the parent's body (found in most mammals, some shark, amphib-

nearest mainland in South America that land birds reached them only very occasionally. The prize for the first species that managed to cross the 600 miles of ocean and breed on the archipelago was an initial absence of competition - all the food and natural resources which a land

■ Bartolome Island, Galapagos.

Photography: T. P. Littlejohns/WWF

ian and reptile species and in *male* seahorses).

We can also see how speciation is a machine for generating the variety and pervasiveness of life over much shorter time scales and in quite small locations. The classic example is the evolution of the 13 species of finches which are unique to the Galapagos Islands. Charles Darwin visited this remote archipeligo in 1835 and he, along with other crew on HMS Beagle, shot and collected the small birds. The finches helped him to arrive at his theory of evolution through natural selection a few years later. When the Galapagos rose from the Pacific four million years ago they were so far from the

bird could use were its alone. The one which appears to have got there first was a species of finch; it founded the 13 species scattered among the Galapagos today and found nowhere else in the world. The obvious differences between these finches are in the size and shape of their beaks which enable them to follow ways of life normally reserved for quite different types of birds on the mainland. Some have slender bills to catch insects and drink nectar from flowers. Others have thick bills, enabling them to follow the normal finch profession of cracking open seeds and fruits with tough outer casings. Two of the species of finch have learnt to feed on insects hidden in holes and crevices deep within wood - the woodpecker's speciality. But instead of smashing their way in with rapid beak blows, like a woodpecker, these Galapagos finches use a cactus spine or a leaf stalk which they hold in their beak and poke into the entrances, winkling out their prey. On two of the smallest and remotest of the islands the finches have taken up vampirism. They peck at the roots of big feathers on large seabirds, making them bleed and then drinking the blood. They also push seabird eggs against rocks to crack them open and eat the contents.

How does it work, this all-important process of one species spawning new ones? Start with the basics of evolution. Take any one characteristic of a population of animals or plants - overall size, the time of year when it breeds, the precise chemical make up of any one of its thousands of different protein molecules - and you will find it varies slightly from individual to individual. That is because the genes - which specify those characteristics and which are passed down the generations - themselves vary, because random mutations keep cropping up in them. Many of these chance alterations in the genes are silent or hidden, making no difference to the physical attributes of the individual in which they occur. When they do make a difference they are usually harmful, so that the individual in which they are expressed never develops as an embryo, dies young or fails to breed. They are weeded out by natural selection which, nearly all of the time, is conservative. Mostly it acts to keep species the way they are rather than to change them.

But very occasionally one of these chance mutations confers some slight advantage on the individual which has it. That small, benign difference means it will have a few more children than its rivals. Its offspring will inherit the superior gene and, as a result, themselves be more like-ly to have more children to which they will pass on the same advantage. With each passing generation the beneficial mutation becomes more and more common in the population until it is the norm. The species has evolved a little.

Now, back to speciation. It is likely that individuals of any one species will be living in a variety of slightly different environments across its range, so an individual which is perfectly adapted for conditions in one locality will be a little off the mark in another. One part of the species' area might be a bit hotter or wetter than another zone, or a different kind of predator or prey might be encountered there. If you think that a single type of plant or animal is often scattered over terrain which is hundreds or thousands of kilometres across then you realise that this situation will be a common occurrence. Next, imagine some sort of physical barrier which splits a species into separate populations which cannot interbreed. This is not unusual; it was exactly the situation which that first finch species faced when it arrived on one of the Galapagos islands and begun breeding there. Finches then spread through the archipelago, but each population on each island bred almost entirely among itself and encountered birds from the other islands only very rarely. Each separate population tended to evolve in different directions to fit itself to the local opportunities and challenges.

Now imagine that this physical barrier separating two populations of one species is removed. The sea level might fall, establishing a land bridge between two islands. Or, for a species living in woodlands, two separate patches of forest might merge as trees grow up in the grassland between them. The two groups which have evolved apart meet and mingle - but they no longer interbreed. Their mating seasons might have changed, or their appearance or behaviour have altered to the point where males and females of the two different groups no longer recognise each other as prospective mates. In that case there is no longer any flow of genes between the two groups; they have already separated. Speciation has occurred; one species has given rise to two which will forever follow separate evolutionary paths.

But consider the situation in which the two groups from one species meet again and can and do still interbreed. They could merge back into one species. But if the two groups have become adapted to slightly different ways of life during their time apart then the offspring which come from breeding between them will be perfectly fitted to neither - and will therefore be at a disadvantage. These in-betweens will generally die younger and have fewer children. In that case, any gene which makes it less likely that an individual of one group will mate with a partner from the other group, and more likely that it will stick to its own kind instead, will be good news. Such a gene will give every individual which possesses it the advantage of not wasting its breeding efforts on liaisons which produce inferior children; over the generations it will become the norm. In this way, natural selection can force two different groups within one species apart, accentuating differences and favouring traits which rule out interbreeding. The end result is, again, speciation - one becomes two.

There is still plenty of argument among scientists about the details of this process. One of the biggest debates concerns the extent to which two groups have to be physically isolated from each other for speciation to occur. Any tendency for the two to evolve in different directions will be strongly suppressed by interbreeding between them, yet it seems that a new species can arise without complete isola-

tion from its founder. There is another controversy over why closely related species do not mate with each other. How often is this simply an accident, a by-product of them evolving in different directions, and how often is it the result of natural selection favouring genes which prevent interbreeding?

To further confuse the picture, flowering plants can speciate in the same way as animals but they have extra tricks of their own. One species may found a new species instantly, and two species which do not interbreed can found a new and successful hybrid species. These speciation shortcuts happen when plants double or treble their usual complement of chromosomes, the microscopic strings of DNA and protein which carry all of the genes. About 40 per cent of today's flowering plant species have arisen in these ways.

Nature provides us with many examples of the 'just before' and the 'just after' of speciation. 'Just', in this case, means a few hundred thousand or a few million years, the blinking of an eye on the languid time scale of evolution. But we have next to no examples of the actual moment when speciation occurs. The birth can be imperceptibly gradual, as one population slowly grows different from another, or it can happen in just a few hundred generations. Speciation is inherently difficult to catch in the act. It's much easier to see the process with the benefit of hindsight, when two species have stopped interbreeding for some time and evolved further apart.

Once a successful new species has been founded it will spread outwards, colonising other places and even other continents. Almost all plants and animals have evolved ways of casting their seeds, eggs or young out into the world. You can see why genes which promote dispersal do well. If the young were to mature in the same place as their parents they would compete with them for food and other resources, and a local disaster like a forest fire or a flood would wipe out the entire lineage. Together speciation and dispersal explain why life is so extraordinarily widespread and seizes ever opening, with a different species specialised for each habitat and micro-habitat. As a big, fairly fast moving animal, we see the world in terms of metres and kilometres, but for small animals and plants a distance of a couple of millimetres or centimetres can make all the difference in the opportunities that present themselves. The sunny, southern side of a small rock, the shaded northern side, the dark and humid crevices beneath it will each be home for completely different collections of creatures - as different for them as the different sides of a mountain are for us.

There is one further cause of life's diversity and pervasiveness. As new species are formed and biodiversity rises the expansion provides opportunities for further expansion. The process feeds on itself. Billions of years ago, once the earliest life forms were established, the chance was there for new species to eat or parasitise them...and it was grabbed. Today, there are many individual species which have hundreds of other species completely dependent on their existence - because they provide food, shelter, sanctuary or some other crucial resource. Just one tree species in a tropical rainforest can have more than a hundred different kinds of beetle entirely dependent on it - they are not found on any other tree species. Apart from the beetles, which are thought to be the most diverse category of being, there will be numerous other insects and small creatures which specialise in living on and eating that tree - or other things that live on it. Our own kind, *Homo sapiens*, has myriad varieties of life which have evolved to live in or on us - bacteria, viruses, lice, mites and worms. These tight links between quite different kinds of life are not always exploitative; close co-operation has paved the way for thousands and thousands of new species. Think of the panoply of lichens, in which algae and fungi live entwined together, or all of those flowers and the insects and hummingbirds which pollinate them while gaining nectar.

How can we begin to size up this diversity? We have only the vaguest ideas about how many different species there might be on earth today. We do not even know how many we know. The latest United Nations Environment Programme estimate is that about 1.75 million have been discovered and described by taxonomists - scientists who classify life - but this is very rough and ready. More than half these known species are insects.

One reason why this 'known' number cannot be pinned down is that it keeps rising. Scientists are still discovering new kinds of large, fairly visible animals such as mammals and birds; each year a few are found in some distant rainforest, savannah or island. As for the really diverse groups of living things, such as flowering plants and insects, the number of novelties identified each year runs into thousands. In total about 36 new species are identified every day.

No one organisation or nation keeps a single, frequently updated list of all the species. Instead the rising volumes of data (and specimens) are divided among thousands of individual specialists, university departments, natural history museums, botanical gardens and esoteric periodicals. Even if all this information was brought together and kept up to date in one large library or database it would still be inadequate, for it would cover only that minority of the total number of species which have been discovered. There are estimated to be between 3.6 and 112 million out there, with the UN Environment Programme's "working assumption" put at 13.6 million. These meganumbers have been arrived at by various routes; sampling and surveys in diverse nations and habitats and a growing theoretical knowledge about how many species can live side by side. Scientists' confidence in their estimates of total numbers changes dramatically between the different kinds of professor who is one of the world's foremost experts on the diversity of life, says bacteria are "the black hole of taxonomy". Microbiologists have identified some 4,000 species but clever experiments have indicated that in a single pinch of soil there are thousands of as yet unidentified species.

To baffle us further, there are all the species that have been and gone during

How many species are there ?

Described (known) species		Number of estimated species		Working figure	Accuracy
		High Guess	Low Guess		
Viruses	4,000	1,000,000	50,000	400,000	Very Poor
Bacteria	4,000	3,000,000	50,000	100,000	Very Poor
Fungi	72,000	2,700,000	200,000	1,500,000	Moderate
Protozoa	40,000	200,000	60,000	200,000	Very Poor
Algae	40,000	1,000,000	150,000	400,000	Very Poor
Plants	270,000	500,000	300,000	320,000	Good
Nematodes	25,000	1,000,000	100,000	400,000	Poor
Arthropods					
Crustaceans	40,000	200,000	75,000	150,000	Moderate
Arachnids *	75,000	1,000,000	300,000	750,000	Moderate
Insects	950,000	100,000,000	2,000,000	8,000,000	Moderate
Molluscs	70,000	200,000	100,000	200,000	Moderate
Vertebrates **	45,000	55,000	50,000	50,000	Good
Others	115,000	800,000	200,000	250,000	Moderate
Totals	**1,750,000**	**111,655,000**	**3,635,000**	**13,620,000**	**Very Poor**

* Spiders, Scorpions, Mites, Etc.

** Fish, Amphibians, Reptiles, Birds, Mammals

Source: Global Biodiversity Assessment
UN Environment programme

life. They are fairly confident that most kinds of vertebrates - mammals, birds, reptiles, amphibians and fish - have already been identified, and that the actual total lies between 50,000 and 55,000 species. They feel pretty sure there are no more than 500,000 different kinds of higher plants, even though only 270,000 are known. But for some life forms such as fungi, molluscs, nematodes (tiny worms) and the bacteria and viruses which can only be seen under the most powerful of microscopes, there are only hazy guesses about what colossal numbers might exist. E.O Wilson, the Harvard the past three billion years and more of life on earth. We know that extinction is an utterly routine affair in nature, with individual species rarely lasting more than a dozen million years. More than 95 per cent of those which have ever existed have departed into eternal night and only a tiny minority have left fossils for us to find, prise out and ponder.

Chapter Two

THE RISE AND FALL OF BIODIVERSITY

There have been times when extinction has been anything but routine, when unthinkably chaotic and destructive cataclysms have wiped out half or more of all the life on earth. The fossil record reveals five of these extinction spasms during the 600 million years or so since complex, multicellular animals first evolved from simple, single-celled forms, along with several smaller hiccups. The greatest of these diebacks was at the end of the Permian era 245 million years ago, when at least nine tenths of earth's entire complement of species seems to have vanished. The most recent was at the end of the Cretaceous era 65 million years ago, when the dinosaurs and much else disappeared.

Ice ages and other huge shifts in climate, changing sea levels, successive volcanic eruptions poisoning the air and blocking out the sun and the impact of gigantic meteorites several miles across are the best of the many explanations on offer for these mass extinctions. After a decade of fierce debate the cosmic collision theory remains the favourite for the catastrophe at the end of the Cretaceous. A likely site for a rogue asteroid's impact crater has been found, buried beneath the Caribbean seabed off southern Mexico. The impact, at a speed of tens of thousands of miles per hour, would have instantly erased all life for hundreds of miles around it, sent tidal waves crashing dozens of miles inland, thrown up enough rock dust and started enough forest fires to plunge

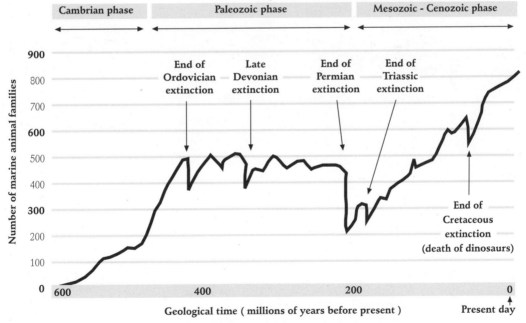

Source: J.J. Sepkoski - Systmatics, Ecology and the Biodiversity Crisis, Columbia Universcity Press, 1992

Previous mass extinctions which have interrupted the steadily rising trend in biodiversity. The graph above shows the changing number of families of marine animals known from fossil record over the past 600 million years. (A family is a level of classification higher than a species and genus but below an order and class. Our own species, *Homo sapiens*, belongs to the family Hominidae which includes the other, now extinct man-like apes. This family is itself part of the order of Primates, which includes all monkeys, apes, lemurs etc.)

entire oceans and continents into darkness for months.

Life recovered its diversity after each of these disasters, but the fossil record tells us that each time it took ten million years or more. We are now living in the middle of another such cataclysm which has a new and quite different cause. The absolute, unprecedented dominance of one species - us - is putting the existence of a large proportion of all other life in jeopardy.

Since 1600, 611 animal species and 654 plant species have been recorded as going

lasts for roughly a million years. That implies that of the 5,000 or so mammal species estimated to be alive today, we would expect just one to become extinct naturally every 200 years. Yet we know for certain that 86 mammals have disappeared since 1600. So for furry, warm blooded, milk-producing life the extinction rate in modern history is 40 times quicker than nature's.

For life as a whole that is an underestimate; the pace of species death today is hundreds or thousands of times faster than is natural. We know that, because in recent decades the tropical forests, the

Recorded number of extinctions since 1600			
Group	Totally Extinct	Extinct in the wild (but survives in capticity).	Total
Mammals	86	3	89
Birds	104	4	108
Reptiles	20	1	21
Amphibians	5	0	5
Fishes	81	11	92
Molluscs	230	9	239
Crustaceans	9	1	10
Insects	72	1	73
Other invertebrates	4	0	4
Plants	654	-	654
Total	1,265	30	1,295

Source: IUCN - The World Conservation Union
World Conservation Monitoring Centre 1996

extinct; that, at least, was the count in late 1996. They were named, described, and then vanished, in most cases during the last 100 years. Not one of the these disappearances seems to have been an entirely natural event; each time humanity played a part, and usually a very obvious one.

A little more than 1,200 extinctions out of the 1,750,000 species known to science seems trivial, but try looking at these figures another way. The fossil record stretching back over tens of millions of years suggests that each mammal species

habitats which alone harbour half the earth's species, have been losing between half a per cent and two per cent of their area each year - which implies that *two species become extinct every hour*. The forests are being replaced by scrub or farmland which supports far fewer species.

We'll return to that extinction rate in a moment, but first let's ask why the rainforests are so extraordinarily rich in wildlife. One hectare in the Amazon can often have over 200 different species of tree and sometimes over 400, while in an

■ View of Korup Rainforest, Cameroon.

Photography: P. E. Parker/WWF

ancient British forest you would be lucky to find much more than a dozen in the same area. Four reasons are put forward, mainly because they can also explain why quite different habitat such as coral reefs also has high biodiversity.

The first is economic, but the economy we are dealing with involves energy, not money. At the bottom of almost all food chains (or rather food webs, because there are cross connections) are plants, which use solar energy to turn water and carbon dioxide into food - stored chemical energy which they need to live from day to day, to grow and reproduce. Animals eat plants, and in doing so much of this stored chemical energy passes to them - they need it for the same reasons as the plants. Then there are the carnivores which eat these herbivores. And right at the top of the food webs are a small number of top predators which specialise in eating other carnivores, like the killer whale which hunts the seals which hunt the salmon and cod which catch smaller fish which eat tiny crustaceans and other minuscule animals which eat the planktonic, single celled plants. The chemical energy that is passed up the food webs diminishes at each stage; a large chunk is wasted each time one creature eats another. That is why the top predators are so thin on the ground (and in the sea). But consuming some of the waste is an under-rated army of scavengers, eating all the bits of dead plant and animal and dung - creatures as diverse as woodlice, mushrooms, earthworms and soil bacteria.

The more sunny, warm and wet it is, the more chemical energy plants can make and store. The rainforests offer just about the greatest combination of warmth and high humidity found on dry land, and while they are often cloudy there is plenty of sunshine too. So these forests have among the biggest natural economies of all habitats, allowing a great diversity of species to divide up all that wealth between them.

The second reason for the rainforests' species richness is stability. They are ancient habitats where evolution and speciation have had plenty of time to build

have survived when the forests joined together again.

The fourth reason is area. Rainforests are

■ Scots Pine Forest in winter - the natural economy goes into recession.

Photography: P. J. Banks/WWF

up biodiversity. In places nearer the poles, like Britain, life has only had about 10,000 years since the end of the last ice age in which to reclaim the land. Furthermore, there is something about the seasonal extremes found in temperate climates like ours which keeps the variety of species down. During our cold, dark winters the natural economy grinds almost to a halt and animals and plants need special strategies to cope such as migration, hibernation and shedding their leaves.

The third explanation is fragmentation. It's possible that in the past few 100,000 years great rainforests like the Amazon's were split into many, smaller forests with open country separating them. Climate change and huge forest fires may have caused this. In each fragment different species would have evolved, as we saw in the previous chapter, and many would

huge. The larger an area of habitat is, the more species it can support; this is a fundamental law of ecology. This relationship between species richness and area is complex; it varies according to the type of life we are looking at (flowering plants, say, or birds), the type of habitat in question and the nearness of other patches of the same kind of habitat which can provide new arrivals, colonists, to replace those species which become locally extinct from time to time. The subtleties of this species-area link and the reasons for it are hotly debated among biologists, and so are the exceptions to the law. But, broadly, it holds and for the rainforests the law suggests that for each one per cent of their area lost - which is roughly what is happening each year - one quarter of a per cent of their species become extinct.

That sounds a very small proportion but look at the numbers which flow from it. Assume there are seven million rainforest species - half of the total estimated for the entire planet (the actual number in these forests will certainly exceed a million, and may be above ten million). If a quarter of rare and threatened, based on surveys of their populations. The centre uses three main levels of threat; vulnerable, endangered and critically endangered. Those in the last category are in deep trouble, teetering next to the abyss of extinction. Of the world's known mammal species 25

Numbers of threatened species

Threatened	Critically Endangered	Endangered	Vulnerable	Total threatened as a percentage of all known species in each group
		THREATENED		
Mammals*	169	315	612	25%
Birds*	168	235	704	11%
Reptiles	41	59	153	-
Amphibians	18	31	75	-
Fishes	157	134	443	-
Invertebrates	358	405	1,128	-
Plants**	-	6,019	8,000	-

* A full assessment has only been done for mammals & birds
**The categories used for plants are not identical to those used for animals, but they are broadly comparable.

Source: World Conservation Monitoring Centre 1996

a per cent of them become extinct each year that means 17,500, or *two each hour*. With the passing of time the small proportion lost per annum also mounts up. After 50 years, one eighth of all species will be extinct. After 100, over a fifth will have gone forever. E.O.Wilson forecasts that over the next century a quarter will become extinct if we carry on destroying habitat at today's pace.

These crude estimates are based on theory, several assumptions and just one type of habitat, the rainforests. Remember, too, that we are talking mostly about the loss of species which have not even been discovered (and, of course, never will be). There are however, further facts about threats to known species which suggest these dismal estimates are quite reasonable and cannot be dismissed as scaremongering.

The job of the World Conservation Monitoring Centre in Cambridge is to compile data on endangered species and habitats. In 1996 it declared that 5,205 animal species and 33,730 plants were per cent were in one or other of the categories and 4 per cent were in the worst of them, critically endangered. The rate at which mammals and birds have been moving through these rankings, mostly coming nearer and nearer to the brink as populations dwindle, suggests that if present trends continue half will be extinct in the wild within 300 years, according to the 1995 Global Biodiversity Assessment, a 1,100 page report written for the United Nations Environment Programme.

So there is absolutely no escaping it; we are well into the earth's sixth great extinction spasm. It seems to have started tens of thousands of years ago, before agriculture and civilisation. Modern man, the world's most lethal top predator, had become an intercontinental wanderer fanning out over the globe and hunting large game. Soon after the arrival of humans in Australia 30,000 years ago and in the Americas in 12,000 BC several species of large mammal disappeared. More recently, the Polynesians have spread from South East Asia across the Pacific, colonising island after far flung island with their heroic deep sea voyages. The arrival of their canoes signalled death for many mammal and bird species which were unique to islands like Hawaii and New Zealand.

Then, in the last 500 years, came the

is the destruction of natural habitats due to the colossal, fast growing human population needing more and more space. Half of the earth's land surface outside of the ice caps has already been turned into crop fields, ranch lands, cities and forestry plantations. Think back to the natural

■ Burnt rainforest for ranching, Amazonia, Brazil.

Photography: Mauri Rautkari/WWF

Europeans, transforming societies on every continent and sharply accelerating the destruction of natural habitats. Now, for the first time, humanity precisely recorded and committed to history the extinctions it was causing - the Dodo in 1681, the Great Auk in 1844. The bulk of these documented disappearances involved creatures living on remote islands. These are places with a life of their own, dozens of species which have evolved in isolation. The larger island animals proved fatally unafraid of human hunters, while the alien predators which the sailors and settlers brought with them, such as rats and cats, ate much of the local wildlife out of existence.

Today the greatest threat to biodiversity

economy in which the primary wealth creators are the plants using sunshine, carbon dioxide and water to make stored chemical energy. On land, 40 per cent of that energy is now estimated to go to us and our farm animals and factories.

Everyone has heard about the dwindling rainforests of South America, Africa and South East Asia. In some the mainstay of destruction has been the international timber trade. The loggers may take only the largest of the trees but their roads and paths help settlers to come in, clear the lower growth and begin farming. In the Amazon loggers and their chainsaws, while far from blameless, have played a lesser role. The forest has been cleared mainly to stake land claims and because of often failed attempts to ranch cattle and grow crops on the poor soils.

But of course it's not just the rainforests which are shrinking. So are the dry tropical forests and the much smaller areas of primeval forests which have survived in cooler climates in the USA, Canada and Siberia. So are the savannahs and other

lations need more meat from the bush but often it is international trade which fuels the demand - for ivory and rhinoceros horn, for very scarce and extraordinarily colourful parrots which are sold at extraordinarily high prices, for the tiger bones, bear gall bladders and seahorses used in the booming global market for traditional Oriental medicines. You can

Fire Coral and Moorish Idols, Sulu Sea, Philippines.   Photography: Jack Jackson/WWF

wild grasslands, the wetlands and the mangrove swamps. Coral reefs, the sea's equivalent of tropical rainforests, are dynamited, polluted and smothered by sediment which rainwater washes down from deforested lands.

The next greatest threat to life after habitat destruction comes from over-exploitation of wild species. Continental shelves the world over are overfished and huge numbers of sea mammals, seabirds and unwanted fish are caught accidentally then flung back over the side, dead. On land, many of the larger animals in the remaining natural habitat are over-hunted or over-collected. Growing local popu-

find these medicines on sale in Europe and North America as well as across South East Asia. They are believed to relieve all manner of ailments and to increase sexual potency, and some probably work. But the growing trade has brought several scarce animals, including the Siberian tiger - largest of the great cats - to the edge of extinction.

Human population growth, one of the main engines of this mass extinction, is forecast to level off midway through the next century. Hopefully by then most countries will have standards of living at least equal to those the West enjoys today - high enough to allow societies and

Governments to afford to conserve wild habitats and species if they want to. But the economic development and industrialisation which should provide this wealth are themselves certain to do serious damage to biodiversity. Coal, oil and gas, the buried remnant of plants and animals living tens of millions of years ago, form the lifeblood of modern economies. Growing consumption of these fossil fuels is raising the atmospheric concentrations of carbon dioxide and methane in the atmosphere, and so is the burning of tropical forests. These gases trap more of the sun's warmth in the lower atmosphere, raising temperatures and sea levels and altering climate.

It's likely that in the next century some

harm. Species and habitats will be severely tested by a pace of climatic change which is forecast to be the fastest since the last Ice Age abruptly ended 10,000 years ago.

Climate change is nothing new; wildlife has been challenged by entirely natural swings in climate many times in earth's long history. Species coped by moving to areas where there were climatic conditions they were adapted to. But it becomes much harder to make such long journeys if, say, you are a forest species confined to small islands of surviving woodland surrounded by seas of farmland. And if you are a tree facing climate change you cannot move at all; you have to spread your seeds in the hope that

■ Salt marshes in Britain, at risk from rising sea levels.

Photography: J. Plant/WWF

coastal, freshwater wetlands will be flooded by sea, while natural habitats surviving further inland will be destroyed by people forced to abandon their homes and fields close to the shore. Higher temperatures, changes in rainfall and shifts in the prevailing wind may do as much or more

some will reach a place where they can grow.

Acid rain, which is also caused by the burning of fossil fuels, is another threat. Across swathes of Europe and North America where there are soils and rocks which cannot resist - or 'buffer' - acidity, much of the life in lakes and rivers has been killed. On land the types of plant species found in natural habitats can be much altered by acid rain and varities sometimes disappear. The developed nations are now curbing this pollution, reducing the sulphur and nitrogen emissions from power stations, vehicles and oil refineries which turn rainwater into dilute acids. But as India and China consume their huge coal reserves air pollution's shadow will darken over wildlife-rich South East Asia.

So habitats and species will continue to disappear into the next century, probably at an accelerating rate. Why should we worry about this, and fight to slow destruction's tide? After all, we know that nature is careless and heartless with its own and that the great majority of species ever to have lived have gone extinct. We know that there is a fantastic abundance of life and that even if present trends continue there will still be plenty left in 50 years time.

There are several reasons to fight, and most involve humanity's self interest. But let's start by considering what we do when we cause a single species to become extinct. Do not be fooled by *Jurassic Park*; we destroy it forever and there is no way to bring it back. We eliminate an end product of nearly four billion years of evolution on earth, an entity with an incredibly long and eventful history which is adapted for its own particular way of life in a space which can range from a small island to an ocean or continent. Even if you have no religious beliefs and feel the universe is the product of blind, impersonal forces, you still have to recognise the uniqueness of each species, be it however small and dull. It represents order flowering in the face of chaos. You could say that each pebble on a beach, each grain of sand, is different from the others and has a history going back to the formation of the earth - but, unlike a species', its uniqueness is trivial and boring.

Our children and grandchildren won't

■ Camel Cycle Trail, Cornwall. - nature for all.

Photography: J. Plant/WWF

thank us for wiping out wildlife, wilderness and semi-wilderness, and we have no right to deprive them. We need these things and so will they, to help keep us sane and content and to provide us with beauty, inspiration and tranquillity. Why do we love nature so much? Why would even the most urban of us, who cannot identify any birds apart from pigeons and sparrows and who shudder at the thought of muddy walks in deep countryside, want to defend rainforest and reef, savannah and swamp? Is it God-given, or part of our own evolutionary make-up, or both? Our longing for views of open countryside and water, our fascination and fear for other species, are probably stitched into our genes. The thought of having to depend more and more on television and virtual reality programmes for access to nature while the real thing fades away is a deeply unpleasant one.

There are other self-interested reasons for wanting to slow the loss of biodiversity. We depend on just 20 different species of plant for 90 per cent of the world's food. The list is led by wheat, rice, barley, maize and potatoes. In an increasingly crowded world in which the fertility of farmland soils is abused we will need to find new food species, or wild ancestors of the varieties we grow now. For instance, crops which can tolerate soil with high salt levels will be useful for the huge areas of land which have been salinised - made salty - by irrigation schemes. So will varieties which are resistant to drought and new diseases. A wild species of wheat found in Turkey has genes which gave the domesticated plant resistance to disease; in doing so it is estimated to save farmers around the world about $30m a year. Unknown genes which humanity could one day exploit are out there in the wild, because plants and animals have had to face such a huge diversity of challenges during their evolution. Now that genetic engineering allows us to move genes

between species which are not closely related those wild genes become more exploitable.

Food is not the half of it, for humanity has always found many other uses for wildlife. It has been estimated that there are between 25,000 and 30,000 different plants which have been used for medicinal purposes by different peoples around the world. In the United States a quarter of all medicines dispensed were originally derived from plants, or still are. One celebrated example of a medically useful wild plant is the rosy periwinkle which is widespread in the tropics. It contains two chemicals, vinblastine and vincristine, which combat two cancers - Hodgkin's disease and acute lymphocytic leukaemia. Sales of the drugs derived from it bring in tens of millions of pounds a year.

It is not just individual plant, animal and bacteria species which can have great value. Entire ecosystems - the complex of species living in a particular habitat - are often doing us an enormous, unrecognised favour. The sea is kept from eroding and invading the land by sand dunes and the vegetation which ties them down, and by salt marshes and great forests of kelp (seaweed) just offshore which absorb the energy in waves. Forests and other vegetation prevent soil erosion, and in the tropics the rainforests actually help to make the rain by rapidly recycling what falls back into the atmosphere.

There is, then, a powerful case for conservation. Seen as a whole, the sixth great extinction spasm which humanity has embarked on looks insane. But poor people struggling to feed their children do not look at the big picture; they see the urgent need for the money or food they can gain from clearing a patch of forest. Organisations like the World Wide Fund for Nature (WWF) and most conservationists now say it is essential to give local communities a stake in saving their local wildlife and wilderness, otherwise it won't happen. The alternative approach - fencing off reserves and national parks and telling farmers, woodcutters and hunters to get out and stay out - has been tried. It usually does not work in Third World countries. According to the United Nations Environment Programme, 6.3 per cent of the earth's land surface has been given some sort of formal, protected status but in many of these supposed wildlife refuges the pell-mell destruction goes on.

How can local people be given reasons for conserving habitats and species? In many places they already have them, for they have lived in the area for generations and rely on using the natural resources sustainably. Conservation today means defending the rights of forest dwellers from business interests and governments which see a quick profit (and, sometimes, a fat backhander) in clearing the trees. It means helping to find and build markets for natural products from the wilderness, fruits, nuts, fibres and gums as well as wood, and ensuring that local people and their children have a long term right to extract those products - for that gives them an incentive to preserve the habitat. Ecotourism, which is growing fast, can also give local communities a stake in preserving natural habitats, provided some of the money the visitors spend when they tour the rainforest or safari park reaches the locals.

It is, alas, inevitable that much more wilderness and many species will be lost in the next century. But the pace of destruction has to be slowed and the remaining habitats looked after in a way which maximises their benefit to wildlife. At the same time, there are huge areas of damaged, degraded habitat which can be restored at fairly low cost. In some places nature is already doing the job for free, regrowing forests on abandoned farm-

land. The developing countries, home to most of the planet's biodiversity, need help from relatively wealthy countries like Britain to do these things. It does not need to consist entirely of foreign aid (and bad aid schemes have often done great harm to wildlife and human communities). Private sector investment which helps economic growth without damaging the environment is just as important. So is the work of conservation organisations like WWF, which convert the concern and generosity of ordinary people into positive actions.

All of these issues, every concern in this chapter, were recognised at the 1992 Earth Summit in Rio de Janeiro, when prime ministers and presidents from more than 150 nations - representing almost the entire human population - signed the UN's Convention on Biological Diversity. (US President George Bush did not sign, but his successor Bill Clinton put his name to it a year later). This treaty came into force 18 months after the summit, once 30 countries had ratified it. It is the most wide ranging, best-supported international agreement on conserving species and habitats so far. It says all of the right things.

Unfortunately it says them in only the vaguest of terms; it is an extremely weak agreement. There are no sanctions against countries which break the treaty, and even if there were it would be very hard to prove that a nation was in breach. This is because whenever the document binds any of its signatories to actually doing something, it prefixes this with the weasel words "as far as possible and as appropriate". That phrase could be used to excuse almost any failure to conserve habitats and species.

There's worse. During the negotiations which produced the treaty there were long arguments between rich and poor nations over three issues and the final document resolved none of them. The first concerns new discoveries about species and their genes which might prove to be commercially useful (the rosy periwinkle, for example). Third World Government's wanted an absolute guarantee that they would benefit from any such discoveries if the species or gene was found inside their borders; rich countries refused to concede this. The second argument is over transferring the new skills and knowledge of genetic engineering from rich to poor countries. The third is about money; the Third World say it could not be expected to implement the treaty without "new and additional financial resources" from the rich world. But they have not been given any extra money and these days aid budgets including Britain's are being cut. So while all nations agreed on the need to conserve biodiversity, they fell to squabbling about who should pay and who should reap the benefits from exploiting it.

It would be a mistake, however, to dismiss the treaty as a waste of time and paper. It brought all the issues surrounding today's man-made mass extinction into the open. It provides a starting point for further negotiations between countries. And it allows citizens fighting the loss of species and habitats to question and cajole their governments, saying: "You signed this treaty, what are you doing about it?" So, what is Britain doing about it?

Chapter Three

GREY BRITAIN

Eleven thousand years ago Britain looked like Greenland does today. Most of the country was lifeless, covered in ice caps more than a mile thick which stretched down from the north and petered out along a wavy line across North Wales, the Midlands and Norfolk. South of the ice sheets was a frequently frozen tundra like that found today in the far north of Canada and Russia. It supported only a few very hardy plant and animal species.

Then the ice and tundra began to retreat rapidly northwards, and great forests started to grow up over Britain in the mild temperatures which followed the abrupt end of the last Ice Age. Oak, ash, elm and hazel woodlands blanketed England, Wales and southern Scotland, while the northernmost parts were covered in Scots pine and birch. These new forests covered even more of the country than the ice had done a couple of thousand years earlier, but there were still some huge bald patches. The highest mountain tops above the treeline were too cold to support woods There were also marshy river valleys and great estuaries where the ground was too soft and wet for trees and along the coast were long stretches where the unending, uncertain battle for domination between land and sea produced mud flats, sand dunes, lagoons and salt marshes but no ground suitable for forest.

Along with the trees came thousands of plant and animal species, using the broad land bridge which connected Britain to the continent until it was covered by rising sea levels 8,000 years ago. After that, they flew across the North Sea and English Channel, or drifted on the winds. The great majority of our flora and fauna

came from Europe as colonisers since the end of the Ice Age. We have a few dozen species which are unique to these islands and a few which are 'glacial relicts' - clingers on from the long deep freeze which have managed to survive in today's much warmer climes.

People had lived intermittently in Britain for hundreds of thousands of years during interglacials - the warm periods between Ice Ages (one of which we are enjoying now). They had also settled in Britain much more recently during milder, earlier stages of the last Ice Age - until the final advance of its ice caps which preceded the great warming drove them out. Mankind's latest arrival in these islands happened about 6,000 years ago and this time people began to change the land as never before, clearing the great forests with axes to grow crops, to graze their animals and perhaps to aid their hunting. By the time the Romans arrived more than half the woodlands had gone. When William the Conqueror conquered as much as four fifths had been lost. At the end of the First World War the unending demand for extra farmland had left Britain with just 5 per cent tree cover.

Populations of woodland species dwindled with the woods, but the clearances created great opportunities for others. The skylark is believed to have evolved on the steppes of central Asia but this bird of open country was able to build up a huge population in deforested Britain and become an emblem of our countryside. Man's various agricultural uses of the land created and maintained big areas of semi-natural habitats such as the lowland heaths, sheep and cattle-grazed chalk downlands and reedbeds. These were landscapes which endured for centuries and had their own, characteristic wild plants and animals. Even what little forest remained was mostly changed into another kind of semi-natural habitat, the coppice woodlands. In coppicing, the tree is cut down right at the base of the trunk and this causes new shoots to grow up woody and thick the woodsmen cut them off at their base to provide poles and firewood, and the cycle of growth recommences. The felling of the coppice poles lets sunlight and warmth reach down to the woodland floor, allowing plants and animals which would not normally be found in forests to make a living there.

Britain's biodiversity

The terrestrial (land dwelling) and freshwater species in Britain

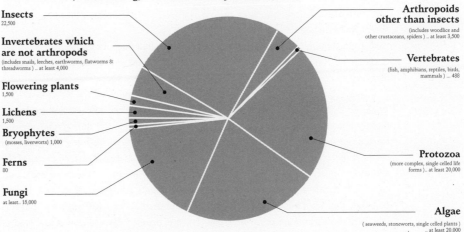

Insects
22,500

Invertebrates which are not arthropods
(includes snails, leeches, earthworms, flatworms & threadworms) .. at least 4,000

Flowering plants
1,500

Lichens
1,500

Bryophytes
(mosses, liverworts) 1,000

Ferns
80

Fungi
at least.. 15,000

Arthropoids other than insects
(includes woodlice and other crustaceans, spiders) .. at least 3,500

Vertebrates
(fish, amphibians, reptiles, birds, mammals) ... 488

Protozoa
(more complex, single celled life forms) .. at least 20,000

Algae
(seaweeds, stoneworts, single celled plants) .. at least 20,000

The terrestrial and freshwater vertebrate species in Britain

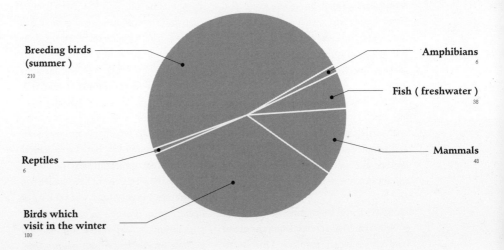

Breeding birds (summer)
210

Reptiles
6

Birds which visit in the winter
180

Amphibians
6

Fish (freshwater)
38

Mammals
48

rapidly from the ground level stump or 'stool'. After a few years, when these shoots have become surprisingly tall, These coppice lovers include several butterflies, wildflowers and the nightingale. But once the tradition of cutting the new growth stops - as it has across most of Britain - the trees grow tall, the canopy closes, the ground is shaded and these species disappear.

Over the centuries people have altered just about every square foot of Britain's land surface, apart from a few remote peaks and cliff sides. They introduced species which in turn influenced other wildlife - the chestnut tree came with the Romans, the rabbit arrived late in the Dark Ages, the invasive, fast spreading sycamore still later. But thousands of years of human use of these islands allowed a wide diversity of wildlife to flourish, around 88,000 species, in a mild, damp oceanic climate with all kinds of underlying rocks and soils. This is not to say that our ancestors were all deep greens and keen conservationists. They hunted the wolf to extinction in Britain sometime in the 17th century. They killed off the beaver, lynx, bear and wild pig even earlier. Fanatical Victorian collectors did serious damage to populations of rare plants and butterflies, while magnificent birds of prey like the red kite, the white tailed eagle and the osprey were driven near to or over the brink of extinction by gamekeepers during the last century.

But this earlier harm to wildlife pales in comparison to the damage done during the 20th century, and especially in the last 50 years. Over 100 plant and animal species are thought to have become extinct in Britain since 1900. Farewell to the orange-spotted emerald dragonfly, which had its stronghold on a river wiped out by pollution from a sewage works in 1951. Good-bye, too, to the burbot, a fish which was also a victim of water pollution in the 1970s, and a small beetle with the scientific name of *Melanotus puncto-lineatus*. Its duneland haunts on the south coast have disappeared under golf courses; it has not been seen since 1986. And let's not forget Britain's vanished plants, either - the hairy spurge in 1924, lamb's succory around 1970 and the sweetly named summer lady's tresses, an orchid which became extinct in Britain in 1959 when the bogs it lived in were drained.

A much larger number of species have also had their populations drastically reduced in the years since the Second World War. The main cause is habitat destruction, the principle reason why bio-diversity is declining around the globe. The British difference is that the habitats being erased are not virgin wilderness but man-made, semi-natural ones. Chief culprit is the intensive modern farming which results from steadily advancing technology and the drive to grow more and more food, thanks to decades of generous subsidies from the taxpayers and food consumers. Between 1932 and 1984 97 per cent of the old hay meadows and pastures found on a wide variety of soils and landscapes - upland and coastal, alkaline chalk and acid peat - have mostly gone. Some have been converted into 'improved grassland', dosed with fertiliser to grow grass for silage or to support higher densities of grazing sheep and beef and dairy cattle. They support a few very fast growing grass species. The old meadow flowers are outcompeted and die back and so do the insects associated with them. Biodiversity withers. The other fate of these species-rich grasslands has been to be ploughed up and turned into cropfields which can produce decent yields on almost any soil, given enough fertiliser, herbicides and pesticides. But these modern, monotonous arable fields with their autumn sowing of cereals, big areas and chemical dependence are deserts for wildlife.

These agricultural changes are the reason why a dozen species of characteristic farmland birds, including the skylark and tree sparrow, have had their populations halved or worse during the past quarter century. These birds are not finding enough food to raise their young or to survive as adults through the winter.

diversity of species. Thanks to this effort, again subsidised by the taxpayers, the tree cover of Britain has been doubled since its low point of 5 per cent at the end

■ Skylark - a victim of intensive farming.

Photography: Robin Williams/RSPB

Intensive farming bears most of the blame, but there are three other causes of habitat destruction. First, the covering of countryside in bricks, concrete and tarmac. Since 1945 about 5,000 square kilometres, an area about three times the size of Greater London, has been built on in England alone, thanks to our unceasing demand for new houses and workplaces - and the shops, schools, hospitals, leisure centres and roads which go with them. Between 1991 and 2016 an area of countryside slightly larger than another Greater London is forecast to be swallowed, taking the proportion of English land which is urban from 10.6 per cent up to nearly 12 per cent.

Second, a huge area of semi-natural habitats has been covered in conifer plantations which support a much lower

of the First World War. But this great tree growing drive has been no boon to wildlife. Most of the new plantations consist of non-native conifers like the Sitka spruce, planted at such high densities that almost no sunlight reaches down through their masses of needles to the ground - so nothing else grows there..

The third cause of habitat destruction is neglect, the abandonment of traditional forms of land management. When farmers stop rough grazing on steep downsides or lowland heaths because it does not fit with modern methods, or when coppicing ceases in a wood because there is no longer any market for the poles, all of these places start the transition towards deciduous forest. This is a fine wildlife habitat and the most natural one for Britain, but it will no longer have the unusual, particular species associated with the semi-natural habitat which preceded it.

Apart from habitat destruction, there are three other reasons for the rapid decline of Britain's wildlife this century:

Over-Exploitation of Natural Resources

Every day in the seas around Britain and Europe there is severe over-exploitation of the fish populations. Fisheries scientists repeatedly warn that too many are caught, at too young an age, creating the risk of a collapse in the stocks due to lack of breeding adults. Only a small minority of cod reach their third birthday. There have been such collapses already this century; North Sea herring remained severely depleted for more than a decade thanks to overfishing.

Another kind of over-exploitation is the rising volume of water taken from underground aquifers by water companies. This has dried out wetlands and left some of England's most wildlife-rich lowland rivers which flow over porous rocks severely short of water, reducing the number of plant and animal species living in them.

Pollution

Effluent from sewage works and the fertiliser running off farmland have over-fertilised much of Britain's freshwater habitats, leaving a reduced diversity of plants and animals able to survive in them. Gross sewage pollution, which still happens from time to time, causes the populations of bacteria which decompose the stuff to explode. They then consume all the oxygen in the water and kill all the fish and animal life. At lower concentrations plant nutrients in sewage effluent and farm fertiliser cause simple, single celled plants - algae - to undergo rapid summertime population growth in rivers and lakes. This turns the water a murky green-brown, sunlight no longer penetrates to the bottom and the more complex, rooted aquatic plants which grow there die. Later in the summer and autumn the algae die back, and their decomposition by bacteria can also produce conditions of oxygen starvation in the water.

Acid rain is caused by the gases which are produced when coal, oil and, to a lesser extent, gas are burnt. These turn the rain, mist, wind and snow downwind of the smokestacks, chimneys and vehicle exhausts acid. When this sour precipitation falls on certain types of underlying rocks - types which are found across much of upland and western Britain - the soils, streams and lakes become acidified. The most obvious effects are seen in the freshwater habitats, and the damage goes back a century or more to the heyday of the industrial revolution. Such streams and lakes support fewer plant and animal species and often the fish have disappeared entirely. In large parts of upland Wales the dipper, a little bird that scuttles around on stream bottoms looking for aquatic insects, has vanished because it cannot find enough to eat.

Acid rain has a more subtle effect on land, altering the composition of communities of plant species on granitic soils which cannot 'buffer' (offset) acidification. Air pollution from the burning of fossil fuels and some kinds of intensive livestock farming - like piggeries - also appears to act as a fertiliser for vegetation, exerting further effects on habitats. Lichens are known to be particularly sensitive to airborne sulphur dioxide which comes from burning coal and oil. Many species have disappeared from large parts of Britain because of it.

Introductions

Species brought in from overseas by accident or on purpose can sometimes do great harm to their native British counterparts. The red squirrel and the freshwater white-clawed crayfish both seem fairly likely to become extinct in Britain in the next century because larger, tougher imports from North America, the grey squirrel and the signal crayfish, are outcompeting them.

Britons have done the worst harm in history to their wildlife during a century in which they have been better educated, more wealthy and more interested in protecting the environment than ever before. Yet this country, more than most, should be setting an example of conservation to the rest of the world. We have a great scientific tradition in advancing the understanding of life. The theory of evolution evolved in Britain, and the relatively young but enormously influential science of ecology owed much of its origins to British biologists. Centuries of close, careful observations of our plants and animals by skilled amateurs and professional scientists mean that we know our flora and fauna, its locations, genetic variation, abundance and migrations, as well if not better than any other country in the world.

And if Britain cannot care for its species, who can? Our land is mostly densely populated and intensively farmed which makes it hard to conserve biodiversity. But most countries will be in that situation in the next century if they are not there already. We in Britain cannot plead poverty as an excuse, for while our place in the economic rankings may have slipped our population is, overall, among the wealthiest ten per cent in the world.

Of course we do care for our wildlife and have done so for centuries; it's just that our concern and our efforts to conserve have always been outpaced by the rate of destruction. Conservation goes back

■ Red squirrel. Photography: Hugh Clark/WWF

longer than written history. When nearly everyone lived off the land there were all sorts of rules and solemn agreements governing the use of shared and private natural resources - who could take firewood from a forest, how much, who could graze their pigs there, how many, and so forth. Medieval kings and wealthy barons kept their own great game reserves private and wooded so that there was plenty for them to hunt. Later, the wealthiest members of society began to create idealised visions of nature in their great landscaped country parks, sometimes moving entire villages when they spoilt a prized view.

the Protection of Birds, were founded just over one hundred years ago amid concern about the loss of countryside and wildlife. Both have grown in membership and influence ever since and are now among the country's biggest landowners. The World Wide Fund For Nature was founded in the early 1960s because big mammals were rushing towards extinction in Africa and Asia, but it now campaigns and helps conserve wildlife and habitats everywhere, including here in Britain.

Successive British governments have had to respond to conservation's massive popularity. In the last 50 years we have had stacks of new laws, policies and official

■ The disappearing mingled landscape of woods, pastures and cropfields created by mixed farming; a mainstay of UK biodiversity for centuries.

Photography: P. J. Banks/WWF

Conservation started to become a mass movement in the 19th century, once most of the rapidly expanding population had moved into cities and was living in squalid conditions cut off from nature and fresh air. Two of Britain's most important conservation charities, the National Trust and the Royal Society for

guidance covering countryside development, protection of individual species and the creation of national parks and nature reserves. A conservation bureaucracy has grown up employing over 2,000 civil servants and Government scientists in more than a dozen departments, agencies and research institutions. Add to that a similar number working for conservation charities, consultancies, local councils and universities and you have an army of experts, administrators and wardens dedicated to wildlife and habitats.

Given all those people, all those laws, all that public support for conservation, why have we failed to stop the tide of destruction? One reason is the sheer pace of change in modern farming; wildlife has never had to face anything quite like it before. Another is that the current system of Sites of Special Scientific Interest, or SSSIs, which underpins much of the Government's wildlife conservation efforts, has proved inadequate in the 15 years since it was introduced.

These sites are designated by the Government because they have rich, rare or unusual collections of plant and animal species. There are more than 6,000 of them and they cover nearly 20,000 square kilometres - or over 8 per cent of the UK's land surface - but most are in private ownership. By law, landowners have to notify the government's nature conservation agencies - English Nature, Scottish Natural Heritage, the Countryside Council for Wales - if they plan any changes or activities which will affect an SSSI. (If they don't do this, and carry out work which damages an SSSI, such as ploughing it up, they can be prosecuted and fined - but the authorities rarely take landowners to court, and when they do the fines handed down are usually modest).

Once notified the agency can then ask the landowner to drop or modify his plans for the sake of conservation and pay him an annual sum in compensation for foregoing whatever it was he planned to do. If the two sides cannot reach agreement and the landowner still wants to go ahead with the damaging activity the Government can step in and order the

landowner not to proceed while further attempts are made to reach an agreement on management of the land and compensation. If that fails then the Government has a legal right of compulsory purchase, although this has never happened since the current SSSI laws came into force in 1981.

The fact is that well over 100 SSSIs are damaged each year and a few are partially destroyed. The law behind them does not crack down on neglect which, as we have seen, can cause a particular habitat to lose the qualities which make it a refuge for rare and endangered species. Nor does it give any guarantee that SSSIs will be protected from damaging developments. Local councils give planning permission for such developments from time to time if they judge that the need for them outweighs the need for nature conservation. Even Government construction projects such as roads sometimes harm SSSIs. The notorious Newbury bypass goes through three of them.

The Government's nature conservation agencies have been trying to modify the flawed SSSI system and make it more positive, giving cash incentives, advice and praise to farmers and other landowners who manage the sites in a way which preserves the characteristic wildlife. But the agencies lack the funds to give every SSSI owner an incentive to care so they are heavily reliant on their goodwill. In a property-owning democracy you cannot compel landowners to look after their wildlife regardless of the cost. Big landowners still have a great deal of clout in our society and they do not take kindly to being told what to do.

You could argue that all the SSSIs in Britain should be taken out of the hands of private landowners and nationalised so that their secure future could be guaranteed. But that is never going to happen.

For one thing, it would cost the Government (and taxpayers) far too much to buy them all. For another, many of the sites are already owned and run by charities and individuals who look after them well. In truth, charities and enlightened landlords have done as much if not more than Government ever has to preserve Britain's biodiversity.

Although recent decades have been the most destructive in history for Britain's wildlife there are reasons to be optimistic, to hope that the tide may soon turn. Both air and water pollution are declining. The planting and management of forests these days is usually far more wildlife-friendly. And while the SSSI system may be inadequate, two important European Union laws should substantially beef up the protection of our best wildlife sites. These laws, the new Habitats Directive and the Birds Directive which preceded it, compel all the EU's member states to designate the most important habitats within their borders and implement regulations and policies which guarantee their protection. That should include ensuring that they are not damaged by neglect. Destructive development can be allowed on one of these Euro-sites, but only if the Government can prove that there are compelling economic and/or social reasons why it should be and provided an equivalent area of habitat is created and protected elsewhere. There is a higher level of protection for sites which are designated because they harbour 'priority' species and habitats. These can only be built on and damaged if this is in the interests of public health and safety. Priority habitats found in Britain include saline lagoons and Scots pine forest.

If Britain's government takes these Euro-laws seriously, and if conservation organisations like WWF keep careful watch to ensure they are obeyed, then they can do a great deal of good. The early signs are

that both will. Already more than one third of Britain's total area of SSSIs have been proposed by Government as 'Euro-sites', or Special Areas for Conservation as they are officially and dully known.

Also good news is Britain's follow up to the Biodiversity Convention and the Rio Earth Summit. It is the fruit of an unprecedented degree of collaboration between the Government and the conservation charities and societies, large and small. Together they set up a 'Biodiversity Steering Group' (yet another not-so-snappy title) which included representatives from the National Farmers' Union, the Country Landowners Association, research institutes and local councils as well as senior Whitehall civil servants and people from WWF, the RSPB and the network of county Wildlife Trusts. After more than a year of meetings the group published a two volume, 400 page report in December 1995 which proposed numerous recommendations for better conservation of wildlife, habitats and the overall biodiversity of Britain. You can buy the documents from Her Majesty's Stationary Office bookshops for a breathtaking £56! Six months after it was published John Gummer, Secretary of State for the Environment, made a formal, written response saying that the Government accepted the main proposals while John Major, the Prime Minister, added that he welcomed the challenge posed by the report. There was back-slapping all around at a grand launch in London's Natural Museum.

So what are these proposals which are so welcome, and which are now official Government policy? There are rather vague plans to increase public awareness and involvement in biodiversity (which, the report admits, "is perhaps a cumbersome and unfamiliar term.") There are recommendations for improving the way the enormous quantities of disparate

British data on species are kept and made available to the public, including the development of a UK Biodiversity Database. Britain has reams and reams of information about where thousands of species are found, gathered over the years by devoted amateurs and professionals. But there are problems in keeping this up to date, accessible, and in its compatibility - using one set of data alongside another when the information has been compiled in different ways.

The steering group's fat report also has recommendations for local biodiversity groups and plans, based at the county or regional level, and a structure of new committees to check whether all their recommendations are being implemented. But the core of the report, the part which aroused all the press interest and will cost the most to achieve, consists of action plans for 116 key species and 14 key types of habitat which are rare or in rapid decline. Each plan has targets and price tags attached. If they are carried out then, with some exceptions, each species and habitat will be stabilised and guaranteed a future - rescued, in effect. The exceptions are a few species which have disappeared from Britain altogether, or which are so rare, obscure and little understood that no one yet knows how to go about saving them. But they, like each one of 116 on the list, were picked using a rational selection process which identified them as being most in need of help.

Most of the species action plans demand more research on where the animal or plant in question is distributed and what its habitat requirements are, and spreading advice to landowners on how to manage their acres in a way which favours it. Both the species and the habitat plans call for improved management of habitats and creation of new areas, with subsidies to landowners for doing this. For the 116

species, the extra costs involved (over and above what is being spent on conservation now) are put at £3.8 million per annum next year falling gradually to £2.4m a year in 2010. The steering group does not say who should pay, but points out that the cost of similar, earlier species recovery plans were shared roughly equally between the Government and voluntary conservation groups. As for the habitat action plans, the extra costs are put at £13m next year rising to £37m in 2010, and the steering group says it expects the Government to meet them.

So we are talking about the Government finding roughly £15m to £40m a year, or at most £1 for each British adult. Let us put these costs in context. The Government already spends almost £100m a year funding its nature conservation agencies (English Nature, Scottish Natural Heritage, the Countryside Council for Wales). It spends £100m a year on 'agri-environment' schemes; subsidies to farmers which pay them to look after their land in environmentally-friendly ways. This is a very small fraction (3 per cent!) of the £3 billion a year of Government subsidies to British farmers under the European Union's Common Agricultural Policy. There is further, smaller, Government funding of nature conservation work through bodies like the Environment Agency and research institutions. And the voluntary sector - organisations like WWF, the National Trust and RSPB, are estimated to also spend about £100m a year on habitat protection and creation in Britain. Put alongside all of these figures, a maximum of £40m a year does not look excessive. It is roughly an extra ten per cent in British conservation funding.

Will the Government cough up its share of the money? Will it implement the action plans? In its official, written response to the steering group's report it

Porpoises.

Photography: Dr Ben Wilson/University of Aberdeen

promised to "give the necessary priority to finding the resources, within the context of overall policies for public expenditure." Overall policies are to keep spending under very tight control, so that could mean little of the extra money asked for being granted or none at all. As for implementing the plans, the Newbury bypass road is still going through prime marshy habitat of the Desmoulin's whorl snail, one of the species on the list of 116 (although the Government is creating, at a cost of many hundreds of thousands of pounds, some new swamp habitat for it nearby). And in the summer of 1996, a couple of months after the Government accepted the biodiversity report, its Scottish Office gave Scottish fishermen the right to use bottom set drift nets off their country's coastline.

These fish nets, which are strung along the sea floor for hundreds of metres and left in place for a day or two, are already known to kill thousands of porpoises, another of the 116 species, each year else-where in the English Channel and North Sea by entangling and drowning them.

This doesn't mean that the Government is totally insincere. It means that it faces conflicting pressures and wildlife and biodiversity will not always get top priority. But now that ministers have signed up to the steering group's report conservation groups are in a much stronger position to condemn any backsliding and broken promises. And bits of the Government, like the Department of the Environment, which want to see the report implemented are more able to demand support (and money) from other parts of Government like the Treasury. It also seems highly likely that a Labour government would accept the report because there was so much consensus behind it.

Beyond the steering group's report lies a broader conservation agenda which is more important still and must never be lost sight of. Our largely urban population has to be kept in touch with Britain's wildlife, to be educated about it and encouraged to appreciate it, but also prevented from loving it to death. The European Union's Common Agricultural Policy has to be reformed so that more of the huge subsidies are targeted towards preserving the habitats we value most. The Common Fisheries Policy also needs extensive change to stop the chronic over-fishing. Finally, we should never forget that the world's greatest biodiversity lies in poor tropical countries where rapid population growth and poverty are combining to erase it. They need our help.

Chapter Four

THE ACTION PLANS

The book looks at 26 of the key species and four of the key habitats in depth, then briefly describes the remaining 90 species and 10 habitats. The Biodiversity Steering Group also called for plans for a further 286 species and 24 habitats to be prepared over the next three years, and the Government has agreed to this.

This is how the key species were chosen. First of all a long list was drawn up, with plants, animals and fungi which met one or more of the following criteria:

Global rarity: their entire global population had to be so low that they were regarded as being in some danger of becoming extinct.

Britain a refuge: the UK had to harbour at least a quarter of their world population,

Rapid population decline: their numbers had to have fallen by a quarter over the past 25 years.

Very patchy and isolated distribution (spatially rare, rather than just having a low population): they had to be present in fewer than 15 of the 2,000 or so 10 kilometre by 10 kilometre grid squares covering Britain.

Legal protection: they had to be protected by UK law or international treaties.

This long list covered 1,250 different types of plants and animals, which were then narrowed down to 400 species using the following criteria; they all had to be either globally threatened or their British population had to have fallen by half or more in 25 years. This was then sieved down to the final list of 116 by choosing those species which met further criteria for being threatened. As a result of all this rationality and logic there are dozens of small, obscure plants, animals and fungi on the list with zero charisma and only 18 birds and mammals, creatures with broad and obvious public appeal. But the otter is there, and while it met some of the criteria it seems to have got through to the final short list purely on grounds of its massive popularity.

A similar process was used to choose the 14 types of habitat. They had to meet one or more of these four criteria: that their area has shrunk rapidly in the last 20 years or that they are now very scattered and rare, that Britain had international obligations to protect them (under wildlife conservation treaties, or European Union law), that they are important for one or more of the 116 key species, and finally, that they have a wider importance for plants and animals which spend most of their lives elsewhere (seagrass beds qualify here, because they are nurseries for baby fish and squid).

What, you may ask, is so special about the 30 species and habitats featured in this book? Apart from the fact that my choice is biased towards the charismatic - you'll find birds, mammals, reptiles and amphibians over-represented - the answer is 'nothing really'. I tried to select a broad cross section which would illustrate the range of threats to UK wildlife.

At the time of writing, the Government was looking for individual organisations including major companies to 'champion' the species - which means funding all or part of the rescue plan's implementation in return for favourable publicity. Around a dozen firms, including some of the major supermarket companies, had shown an interest. A trade union wants to champion the three ant species on the list of 116. The Government also wants conservation groups like WWF UK and some of its statutory agencies to become the 'lead partners' for many of animals and plants, which means taking on the main responsibility for getting the action plan implemented. Inevitably, there were multiple offers to be lead partner for popular species like the porpoise and plenty of activity surrounded them. The action plans are, as I write, already being improved and re-written under the auspices of such bodies as the Water Vole Working Group. But about 50 of the more obscure life-forms - the unfortunately-named depressed river mussel, the Cornish path moss - attracted no champions, no lead partners, no flurry of activity. The Government and conservation organisations had not yet reached any agreement on how to take forward the 14 habitat plans; these will be more expensive and difficult to implement but are arguably much more important.

Since the action plans were written a few of the species have been found in places where they have not been detected in decades, or in locations where they have never been found before. The mole cricket and Desmoulin's whorl snail, for example, seem to be considerably less rare and close to extinction than had been thought. This shows that if you look hard enough, you often find; several of the species may be on the list of 116 simply because we don't know where to find them. However, a species on its way to extinction can often be found to be quite widely and thinly scattered for years. Slowly and fitfully the number of these locations dwindles. Sometimes it reappears in suitable habitats from which it has been absent for years when a few colonisers arrive, but the overall picture is one of decline.

What this suggests is that we need much more data on where the 88,000 or so different species found in Britain are found, and better ways of distributing this information in a readily understood form to people who need or want to know. This was just what the Biodiversity Steering Group recommended but making progress on this front will, quite literally, be a lottery. The Natural History Museum, the Institute of Terrestrial Ecology, the Wildlife Trusts and the Government's Joint Nature Conservation Committee have joined to make a £35m bid to the Millennium Commission the body which grants funds raised by the National Lottery to big projects deemed to have a turn of the century resonance to them. The four organisations want to combine their efforts in biological recording into a coherent whole, available on the Internet and to visitors at 20 locations dotted around the country. It is a splendid idea but as I write it is facing strong competition from many other excellent projects.

Chapter Five
TWENTY SIX SPECIES

BITTERN
Botarus stellaris

The bittern is one of the rarest British birds, with a breeding population totalling less than 50. A handsome, reclusive relative of the slightly larger and more common grey heron, it lives in reed marshes in Norfolk, Suffolk and Lancashire preying on fish, especially eels,

Researchers with the Royal Society for the Protection of Birds (RSPB) now use a computer programme which analyses the frequency patterns in the boom and can tell individuals apart, although a skilled human ear can sometimes distinguish different male birds. The sound also reflects

■ Bittern

Photography: Gerald Downey/RSPB

frogs and occasionally on small mammals and birds.

The golden-brown bitterns are hardly ever seen because they stay among the tall, dense reeds and are well camouflaged. The only way to estimate their breeding population is to listen for the strange, booming calls of the males trying to attract a mate from January to May. It is thought to be the deepest sound produced by any bird, a brief, fog-horn like tone which can be heard up to a mile away.

the quality of the reedbed habitat; a bittern which is happy with its surroundings will boom earlier in the year and louder.

In the summer of 1996, 20 booming males were heard in Britain, the same as last year and up on the 16 detected in 1994. (While a few extra birds were heard at one of the RSPB's large reserves, an important reedbed run by a wildlife trust on the north Norfolk Coast was lost to bitterns when the sea broke through and turned the freshwater saline). But 40 years ago there were more than four times as many and they had a much wider range.

The bittern is endangered in Britain and across Europe mainly due to destruction of its habitat. Large areas of reedbed have been drained and gone under the plough this century. Poisoning by pesticides, harsh winters, sewage pollution lowering fish populations and disturbance by pleasure boating are also likely factors in the bittern's decline. What remains of their habitat in Britain has to be managed to preserve it. Trees and shrubs invade neglected reedbeds and they turn into boggy forests. So the reeds and scrub have to be cut back periodically, and the water table kept high to bring in the bitterns.

Those that breed here already depend almost entirely on nature reserves run by the Royal Society for the Protection of Birds and other organisations for their habitat.

The action plan calls for the bittern's population to be growing and widening its geographical range by 2000, reaching at least 100 booming males over the next quarter-century. This can be done by preserving the 22 remaining large reedbeds where bitterns once occurred and creating 1,200 hectares of new habitat - about four and a half square miles. The RSPB has made a start, purchasing a carrot field in Lakenheath, Suffolk, which will be turned into marshy reedbed. The cost of the bittern recovery programme is put at £10,000 a year.

DESMOULIN'S WHORL SNAIL
Vertigo moulinsiana

Desmoulin's whorl snail is a rare, marsh-loving, slime eating mollusc the size of a large ball bearing which is loved and cher-

ished by some. Soon after it won a place on the list of 116 plant and animal species for which rescue plans had been pro-

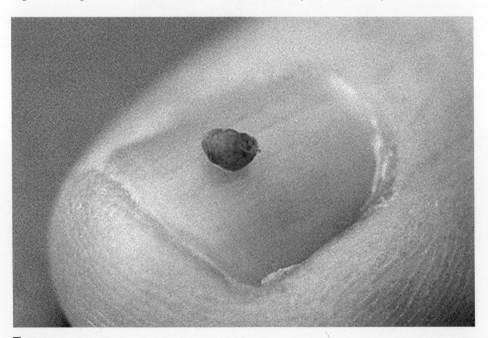

■ Desmoulin's Whorl Snail

Photography: INS

posed, it emerged that the tiny yellow-brown snail lives directly on the path of the controversial Newbury by-pass. Two of its prime sites in Britain, in the valleys of the Kennet and Lambourn chalk streams, are being damaged or obliterated by construction of the £100m road. So the snail became an instant champion of those fighting the bypass. A coalition of environmental and conservation groups went to the High Court to argue that the Government had breached the European Union's Habitats Directive, the EU's most recent and important wildlife law, in failing to declare these two sites to be Euro-nature reserves off limits to development.

They failed - the judge declined to grant the greens a judicial review and the road is going ahead. But the Government's Highways Agency has been forced to spend hundreds of thousands of pounds hurriedly creating alternative, nearby wetland habitat, and to perform the unusual task of moving dozens of square metres of snail-infested reedbed out of the path of the new road and into this new habitat.

The miniscule and declining mollusc lives in the chalky fenlands of southern England, on tall plants like sedges and reeds, grazing on the algal slime which grows on their stems. Conservationists see the whorl snail as an "indicator species" - its presence is the badge of well preserved fens on chalk rocks. The wide-spread draining and destruction of fens has caused its decline and, as the rescue plan points out, their conservation is the key to the mollusc's future. Two other species on the list of 116 live or roost along the line of the Newbury bypass, the pipistrelle bat and the dormouse.

DORMOUSE
Muscardinus avellanarius

The controversial Newbury bypass scheme has created six tiny refugees. These are dormice who lived on the line of the dual carriageway road being built in Berkshire woodland. They had been facing death by concrete and tarmac, but over the past three summers the dormice were trapped by English Nature, the Government's conservation arm, and taken away to safety. Three of them have been retained as captive breeders and three released into the wild in Nottinghamshire.

Why the fuss? There are roughly 500,000 dormice left in England and Wales, but the species is not found in Scotland. Half a million may sound a lot, but this small, golden-brown woodland rodent which weights about the same as two £1 coins has suffered a drastic decline in the past few decades and disappeared from many counties. It seems they are completely unwilling or unable to cross much more than 100 metres of open country. Consequently, the destruction and fragmentation of much of Britain's broadleaved woods has done them great harm. Once a harsh winter or some other mishap wipes out an isolated wood's population the dormice can never return - unless humans intervene to help them.

They are only active at night, climbing high into the tree canopy. They eat pollen, flowers, fruits, nuts and insects, and such a diverse diet requires a fairly diverse type of woodland. They are usually found in coppice woods, ancient woodlands and large old hedgerows. Compared to other mouse species found in Britain, the dormouse is a slow breeder and very long lived - up to five years.

There are other dormouse features which make it quite unusual. Unlike most British mammals, it hibernates - and for a very long time too, seven months, when it sleeps in a shallow underground nest beneath leaf litter. Its tree climbing skills and furry tail also single it out from other mouse species, and so does the relatively long period mothers spend looking after their young. The dormouse is a slow

carefully controlled to prevent in-breeding; English Nature keeps tags on individuals using an official dormouse studbook. In 1996 dormice were re-introduced to Cheshire woodlands after an absence of nearly 100 years.

The action plan for the dormouse calls for its population to be maintained in all counties where the species is still

■ Dormouse.

Photography: Hugh Clark/WWF

breeder, having four to six babies at each birth but never more than two broods in one summer. The young are born and raised in nests in tree holes or in a cozy, grapefruit-sized nest built in low shrubbery and lined with green leaves and honeysuckle bark.

Four years ago English Nature, the Government's wildlife conservation arm, began a species recovery programme for the dormice. This involved breeding some in captivity to provide a stock which can be released in counties where they have disappeared. Who mates with whom is

found, and to re-establish it in at least five where it has been lost. The plan makes it clear that road building is a particular threat to dormice because it breaks up their habitat. It calls on forest owners lucky enough to still have the little mammal on their land to manage their woods in a way which maintains the mouse, and for tree planting and growing grants to tailored for its needs. The maximum annual cost of implementing the plan is put at £60,000 a year.

EARLY GENTIAN
Gentianella anglica

The early gentian is one of many wild-flower species which flourished under traditional farming methods but have been almost obliterated by modern practices. After decades of decline, it is now recorded in only 49 thinly scattered 10 km squares from Cornwall in the south-west to Lincolnshire in the northeast. Botanists chart the abundance of all kinds of plants across Britain by dividing the country up into these squares.

The early gentian is not only rare but highly unusual in that it is found only in Britain; of some 1,500 flowering plants found in these islands only 14 species are similarly isolated. It grows up to six inches tall and has small, delicate leaflets. A biennial, it germinates in late spring from the seed and grows only small leaves in its

■ Early Gentian

Photography: © P. Wakely/English Nature

first summer. These die back to a single, underground bud in the winter which starts growing again early in the spring. Between late May and early June it puts out pink, trumpet-shaped flowers, makes seeds and then dies. Other members of its family are popular garden flowers.

The early gentian requires fairly exposed conditions, sloping ground and shallow soil on chalk, limestone or sand dunes. Its greatest stronghold is Hampshire and the Isle of Wight. Two of the main reasons for its decline are the ploughing up of grassland and the decline of sheep grazing, which allows scrub to move in and oust the small flower. To add to its problems, the unusually dry springs of 1995 and '96 appear to have knocked back the number of flowering plants.

The action plan for this species proposes that all surviving populations should be safeguarded and that by 2004 the plant should be re-established at 10 sites where it has recently become extinct. The way to do this, according to the plan, is to ensure that land owners know what kind of land management is needed to let the early gentian survive. And more farmers need to take part in the Ministry of Agriculture's Environmentally Sensitive Areas scheme which pays them to use traditional farming methods. Once scrub is cleared the early gentian can reappear on downlands, as it has at Banstead Downs in Surrey, where volunteers from Plantlife, a wild-plant conservation charity, have been clearing shrubs.

The Government has proposed that seven sites across southern England where the early gentian lingers should become Special Areas for Conservation under the European Union's Habitats Directive. That should give it an extra measure of protection. Implementing the action plan for this species would cost up to £23,000 a year, with the money coming from government and voluntary bodies.

GREAT CRESTED NEWT
Triturus cristatus

It's estimated that about 200 colonies of the great crested newt die out in Britain each year. This species of amphibian, largest and rarest of the three kinds of newt found here, is in rapid decline across Europe. It is extremely scarce in Scotland, Devon and Cornwall and absent from Northern Ireland. Yet the UK has among the largest populations of this newt in Europe with colonies thought to be still scattered among more than 10,000 remaining ponds.

It can live as long as eight years and grow up to 16 cms long, with up to half of that accounted for by the sinuous tail. Most of its skin is a very dark greeny brown, but flip it over and you see a spectacular orange-yellow belly with black blotches. This is a warning to predators like birds that the newt is extremely unpleasant tasting. It gets its name from the striking crests which the males develop along their back and tails as the breeding season opens in spring, which is when the adults return to the water from life on land to mate. Newt courtship is an elaborate performance with the male chasing the female, fanning her with his tail and striking poses, finally dropping a small sperm package which she picks up. Each of her eggs is left separately on the leaves of water plants which are then folded over in an attempt to protect them from predators. The newly hatched tadpoles are fish-like, less than a centimetre long and transparent but after three months they have grown to half adult length and have lost the external gills they use to absorb oxygen from the water as a juvenile. They usually start living on land in the autumn (although they sometimes spend their first winter in the water), dispersing hundreds of metres in their first three years before they become sexually mature.In winter young and adults hibernate in damp, frost-free crevices. During the rest of the year they are active at night and their food is insects, worms, the tadpoles of frogs, toads and newts (including their own!) and sometimes even the adults of the other two newt species.

The great crested is thought to have built up a population of millions in Britain thanks to the large number of farm ponds used for watering livestock. But usually it drying out. The modern farmscape around what water remains has also become far less newt-friendly over the past half century. But the good news is

■ Great Crested Newt

Photography: © P. Wakely/English Nature

cannot share these ponds with fish, for they eat its eggs and tadpoles, and it seems to disagree with ducks as well. That rules out lakes and large ponds as suitable breeding habitat. A colony needs a decent area - half a hectare or more - of good foraging countryside around its pond where it can find shelter and food. That can be provided by derelict sites, large gardens, open woodland and pasture, but not by intensively farmed fields. Farm ponds have gone into rapid decline because they are no longer needed, silting up, becoming choked with vegetation and

that when a suitable pond is created the great crested may move in because it is still widespread and because its young disperse widely from where they were hatched.

The action plan calls for newt populations to be established at 100 sites each year for the next five years, by creating new ponds or restoring old ones, removing fish and maintaining the right conditions on surrounding land. The cost; about £90,000 a year.

HIGH BROWN FRITILLARY
Argynnis adippe

Britain's most endangered butterfly, the high brown fritillary, has fallen in number by more than 90 per cent over the past 40 years. Before the Second World War the black, white and golden butterfly was a common woodland species but today there are only 51 small sites where it is known to survive in the UK, although it remains common in southern Europe. Of these 51 sites, only nine were classified as having large butterfly numbers, with more than 200 adults flying at peak periods. The high brown fritillary's UK

growth in their search for grass. In doing so, the bracken is left at just the right sort of density and height to create the warm microclimate which the caterpillars demand. Today, however, the plant is

◼ High Brown Fritillary   Photography: Mauri Rautkari/WWF

strongholds are Dartmoor, Exmoor, Herefordshire and the southern edge of the Lake District. Like several other much-reduced butterfly species (five have become extinct in Britain over the past two centuries) it flourished in traditionally managed woods. Every few years a large part of the wood would be cut for coppice poles, creating sheltered areas where the fritillary's caterpillars could bask in the sun after they hatched in March, and where they fed on the leaves of violets. But coppicing has been largely abandoned, leaving woodland too shady and cool for the larvae.

The caterpillars also need dead bracken to cling to, but not so much that the violets - their essential food plant - are swamped. The right balance is maintained by cattle and Dartmoor ponies which trample the

often controlled with weedkiller. The caterpillar satisfies its craving for warmth in a different way in the Lake District; it is found basking in the sparse vegetation next to outcrops of sun-warmed limestone rock.

The action plan for the high brown fritillary calls for this butterfly to be returned to 10 of the sites from which it has recently disappeared by the year 2005. The wildlife group Butterfly Conservation is finalising proposals for the species which form the basis for the action plan, costed at £21,000 a year. Private landowners, the group says, need to be informed on the needs of the species. If they receive any one of the various Government grants available for woodland and countryside improvement, then that should be conditional on their using butterfly-friendly land-management methods to allow the species to re-establish itself. The fritillary may appear to be a delicate, fussy insect, but little more than half a century ago it was well able to co-exist with humankind; it is we who have changed, not the butterfly.

MEDICINAL LEECH
Hirudo medicinalis

The wild, blood-sucking medicinal leech is clinging on at the edge of extinction. Huge numbers are raised in captivity because it is still used in medicine, particularly to make anti-blood coagulating agents and for plastic surgery. But in the wild the leech, a relative of the earthworm, is globally threatened and in Britain there are only a few small, widely

found it in two. "Every species has a right to exist in its natural habitat," says Martin Gaywood, who looks after the leech for SNH. "The medicinal leech is rather a charismatic species - people are both repulsed and intrigued by them."

It is also found on the Welsh island of Anglesey, Cumbria, and a few sites in

■ Medicinal Leech

Photography: Scottish Natural Heritage

scattered populations left.

Several of these populations are in lochs in Argyll. When surveyors from Scottish Natural Heritage, the Government wildlife conservation arm, went to look for the leech in 1995 at eight sites where it had been previously recorded they only

southern England. Its stronghold is on the great shingle spit of Dungeness where shallow ponds harbour it. The total UK population only amounts to a few thousand. The species needs warm (and therefore shallow), nutrient rich and fairly still freshwaters with abundant water plants. The two inch long adults are hermaphrodites, with both male and female sexual equipment, and they lay egg-containing cocoons in the late summer. In the following spring tadpoles are an important food source for the young leeches.

The medicinal leech is much larger than all but one of the other dozen leech species found in Britain, and it also has the most catholic diet - it will attach itself to mammals (including us), birds, amphibians and fish. It swims towards a source of movement in the water, inserts its sucker, injects a little anti-coagulant and drinks deep, taking up to five times its own body weight in blood. Once full it drops off and lies low, spending the next few weeks or even months digesting the meal.

Collection for medicinal purposes may have been an important bygone reason for its decline in Britain and elsewhere (although this may also be how it arrived here from Europe in the first place). More recently, the rapid loss of once widespread farm ponds is an important cause. And some small lakes where they were once found have been deepened to provide the cold water conditions needed by trout, eliminating the warmth-loving leech in the process. The rescue plan calls for a nationwide survey to pinpoint its remaining haunts by 2000 and safeguards for all of these. Ponds should be dug near some of these water bodies to provide extra habitat. The maximum annual cost of this programme is put at £17,000.

GREATER MOUSE EARED BAT
Myotis myotis

Since the last British wolf was hunted to death some 300 years ago only one other mammal has become extinct in these islands, the greater mouse eared bat. It was Britain's largest bat, with a wing span more than a foot across. Unusually, it caught beetles and spiders on the ground as well as hunting in the air using echo-location. It was never common here, for the UK is at the northernmost edge of its European range. The mouse eared was only positively identified in Britain in the 1950s, and its population probably never rose to more than a few dozen.

From 1980 onwards, only two males were ever found in the UK. Most years bat conservationists would find the pair hibernating at a winter roost site near Chichester in Sussex, along with dozens of other kinds of bat. One of them failed to turn up in1985; the other was last seen at the roost five years later. And so, two years later, the species was declared extinct in Britain.

Now it has turned up on the list of 116 declining or endangered animal and plant species drawn up by the Biodiversity Steering Group. Since it has already been lost the action plan for the mouse eared bat is rather limited. "Prepare to launch a major conservation initiative should the species re-colonise or be rediscovered," it says. There are no plans to reintroduce the bat artificially from its strongholds in southern and central Europe because the reasons for its extinction here are not fully understood.

But, according to the Bat Conservation Trust, the factors which have wreaked havoc with many of Britain's 14 other resident bat species are probably to blame. Its hunting grounds of ancient, open woodlands and close-cropped pasture have been reduced by neglect and modern farming. Roosting sites in buildings which give shelter to hundreds of bats have been destroyed by demolition, fires and the spraying of wood preservative. Two other British bat species are on the

■ Mouse Eared Bat
Photography: Dr Bob Stebbings

list of 116 - the greater horseshoe and the pipistrelle. The pipistrelle is the most common British bat with around two million in the country, but its numbers are believed to have fallen by 70 per cent between 1978 and 1993. In the last few years the pipistrelle has been found to consist of two separate species living side by side. Their ultrasonic squeaks, which they use like radar to hunt flying insects, are at two different frequencies. One variety predominates on the Yorkshire side of the Pennines and the other on the Lancashire side, but where they live together they do not interbreed.

MOLE CRICKET
Gryllotalpa gryllotalpa

This is an amazing, extraordinary insect; when people encounter it they believe it has somehow arrived from a distant tropical land. It is native to Britain but hardly ever seen here because it is rare and spends 99 per cent of its three year lifespan in tunnels two feet underground.

It is big beast, as long as your index finger, and has huge, shovel-like front legs which it uses for rapid burrowing. Only the males call, by scraping a comb on their hind legs, and they do it in a shaped burrow which has the effect of projecting and amplifying the high-pitched sound. It's very noisy and continuous, sounding a little like a modern telelphone whose synthetic, electronic ring has got stuck.

About 150 eggs, each the size of a small ball bearing, are laid in June or July, and the mother stays nearby to guard them and keep them clear of fungal growths. Once the young crickets reach two centimetres long they disperse and spend the winter buried in a dormant state. Come next May they start to tunnel and eat voraciously, consuming tubers, earthworms and sometimes smaller mole crickets. Once more they hibernate through the winter and in the spring they undergo their final moult and emerge with fully developed wings. The male calls from his burrow in mid-summer for only two or three nights in his entire life and females within earshot - which may be as much as a

experts have become a little more optimistic since then. For one thing, they believe people are far less likely to encounter and report it now than used to happen because much more digging of the ground is done by machine rather than by hand. For another, it

■ Mole Cricket

Photography: Glyn Griffiths

mile away - fly towards him. They mate and the cycle begins anew.

The insect needs soils which are almost always damp (but not bogs), summertime warmth, and an absence of long, freezing spells in winter. It finds these conditions close to ditches, near places where springs seep from the ground, and generally on the edge of wetlands. The mole cricket is found throughout much of Europe, north Africa and western Asia, but is thought to have declined throughout its range. It has certainly become much rarer in Britain, almost certainly because the area of suitable habitat has fallen. Intensive modern farming methods are, probably to blame.

A couple of years ago the cricket was thought to be on the verge of extinction in Britain but

turned up in the summer of 1995 in a suburban garden in Macclesfield. The residents, a Mr and Mrs Hawkins, were at first startled and a little horrified to encounter one crawling along their patio. But after a while they became quite proud of having provided the rare species with a habitat and they were delighted when they heard a male call in the summer of 1996. They appear to have a colony and there are probably several more dotted around Britain, although no one has a clue how many.

The action plan calls for all surviving colonies to be safeguarded by 2000, for breeding colonies to be established in captivity by that year, and - if feasible - to either identify or establish 20 self-sustaining colonies in Britain by 2005. The costs are put at £7,000 a year.

NAIL FUNGUS
Poronia punctata

■ Nail Fungus   Photography: Gordon Dickson

During a warm autumn in the New Forest the dung of the famous ponies becomes spotted with small white, speckled discs. This is the nail fungus, one of the rarest in Europe and so-called because it resembles the head of large nail driven into the dung. It can only grow in the faeces of horses and ponies fed on acid grasslands with no use of artificial fertiliser. It also has to pass through their bowels before it can grow at all. Once fairly widespread in Britain, it is now thought to be almost completely confined to the New Forest in Hampshire. In autumn these discs eject microscopic spores onto the surrounding grass. These spores - or something they change into (no one has yet found out exactly what happens) - has to be eaten by a pony during the next autumn before the fungus can begin to grow in freshly-deposited dung.

This species is one of four fungi for which rescue plans have been proposed by the Biodiversity Steering Group. The action plan for the nail fungus, costed at up to £9,000 a year, calls for it to be restored to ten former sites by 2004, to study what its needs are and maintain its New Forest population. The key requirement is to maintain horse and pony grazing on the right type of pasture.

The forest is also home for another species on the list of 116 rare or fast declining plants and animals, a very rare type of dung beetle. It lives on the damp ground at the edge of ponds and collects and buries cattle dung on which its larvae feed.

NATTERJACK TOAD
Bufo calamita

TWENTY SIX SPECIES

A century ago the natterjack toad was still common across much of Britain. You could find it as close to London as Blackheath. But now the heath is surrounded by suburbs, heather has been replaced by mown grass and the air is heavy with traffic fumes. Here, as elsewhere, the toads have been wiped out by a combination of habitat loss and air pollution. There are only about 20,000 breeding adults left in Britain, scattered among some 40 sites in England and Scotland. It

its insect prey amid sparse vegetation. It is the noisiest British amphibian, with the males' throat swelling up to ping pong ball size to produce a loud croak.

Both heath and dunes have declined rapidly this century. Much of the heaths have disappeared under housing and forestry plantations or been invaded by scrub and bracken, while many dunes have become covered by dense vegetation. Many of the shallow ponds where it

■ Natterjack Toad

Photography: D. Lawson/WWF

had become extinct in Wales.

The species is common in Spain, but in Britain it seems unable to compete with our common toad and frog. The only place where it can hold its own is in sandy habitats like cattle-grazed heaths and dunes. During hot days it buries itself in sand to keep cool. The toad hunts at night, running rather than hopping after

spawns have also gone. Conservationists believe acid rain caused by pollution has contributed to its misfortunes.

But the natterjack can make a comeback, as a pilot species rescue programme run by the Herpetological Conservation Trust has shown. The toads were reintroduced to 13 suitable or formerly occupied sites, including one in Wales. Among these was a fragment of heathland at the Royal Society for the Protection of Birds' country house headquarters in rural Sandy, Bedfordshire. Special, shallow ponds have been dug on the sandy heath, but perversely the adults have moved through half a mile of woodland to take up residence around another pond right outside the RSPB's canteen.

The rescue plan for the toad calls for its numbers to be maintained at their 1970 level at all sites where it is still found, and for it to be reintroduced to at least five more sites. The most important points are to make sure than landowners know what sort of habitat needs to be maintained to sustain the toad, and to encourage them to manage their land in the appropriate way. The cost of implementation is put at £37,000 a year.

NETTED CARPET MOTH
Eustroma reticulata

The netted carpet moth gets some of its name from the distinctive network pattern on its forewings, and not from any propensity to chew rugs. There are several species of carpet moths, so-called because bygone naturalists fancied that they looked like an exotic eastern carpet. In Britain, this particular species is now found at just 11 small sites in Cumbria and two in North West Wales. Its population is known to have plunged in the past 15 years. The inch-wide moth's misfortunes are connected with the decline of the only plant which its caterpillars can feed on, yellow balsam or touch-me-not.

The adults do not emerge from their chrysalis until July, then they mate and lay eggs. This timing ensures the young caterpillars can eat the plant's growing seeds within their pods; a rich source of protein. They are also disguised as these

■ Netted Carpet Moth   Photography: Paul Waring

pods to avoid being eaten by birds. In the autumn the caterpillar becomes a chrysalis, and remains one through the winter and deep into the next summer.

The touch-me-not, its food plant, is a knee-high annual which likes wet ground and just the right quantity of shade. It is an opportunist which grows on bare earth or broken ground in woodland, beside roads, streams, seepages and lakes. It cannot face much competition from other plants. Several factors have knocked back the touch-me-not; streams drying up or being diverted, and road widening and maintenance destroying its habitat. The abandonment of regular, rotational tree cutting and thinning in woodlands has allowed the plant to be shaded out. The huge numbers of tourists to the Lake District have also done it harm, trampling it around footpaths, car parks and picnic sites.

The main objectives of the action plan for this species are to identify the elusive insect's precise habitat requirements by the end of 1997 and to ensure that, by 2000, all the habitats which it could exploit are managed in a moth-friendly way. The maximum costs of implementing the plan are put at £10,000 a year.

A start has been made. Butterfly Conservation, a wildlife charity, is collaborating with the Government's English Nature wildlife arm, Lancaster University and the National Trust which owns most of the sites where the moth is still found.

Together they are carrying out research, hunting for its haunts and starting to manage the right sort of habitat in ways which encourage plant and insect to thrive.

OTTER
Lutra lutra

The otter is storming back into England, according to an exhaustive survey published in 1996. And in making its comeback it is slowly pushing back the much-loathed mink, a pest species introduced from North America. The fish-eating mammal is now found throughout England and on parts of every river catchment. The number of sites where its 'spraints' - droppings - are found has quadrupled in 14 years. Welsh and Scottish surveys show the otter is thriving there too, but it was in England that it suffered its greatest decline. The main causes were hunting with hounds and, most importantly, poisoning by pesticides. By the mid 1960s it had vanished from most of the country.

The latest English survey, organised by the Vincent Wildlife Trust, took field biol-ogist Rob Strachan two and a half years to complete. He walked along 1,200 kilometres of rivers and streams around England, staying in a camper van for three week stretches. In total, he visited 3,188 sites checking 600 metres of bank at each. He was searching for and sniffing their droppings, the only reliable, easily detectable sign of the elusive mammal's presence. And the only easy way of distinguishing them from the foul smelling mink spraints is to use one's nose. "The otter's smell like jasmine tea and new mown hay, a sweet smell with just a touch of fish," says Mr Strachan. The number of spraints is a good indicator of otter population density. The strongly territorial otters often deposit them in prominent places, such as a flat round stone projecting from the water, to make their presence clear to rivals. They also build little mud or sand heaps and leave the dropping on top. The females are thought to employ spraints to signal their readiness to mate.

Being shy, nocturnal and thinly spread, the eel-loving otters are rarely seen in England. But their spraints are now found near the heart of busy towns - along the Exe in Exeter and the Severn in Hereford. "It's quite likely that a male otter can be well hidden and asleep just a few yards from where dozens of people are walking," says Mr Strachan, now based at Oxford University. During the survey he

fastest, populations of the much smaller, more numerous mink have fallen most rapidly.

Otter surveys in England, Scotland and Wales have been run by the trust, a wildlife conservation charity founded 20 years ago. This was its first English survey; two previous ones were carried out by the Government's Nature Conservancy Council in the late 1970s and the mid 1980s. For all three surveys the country was divided into 50 kilometre (31 mile) squares, with the same stretches of riverbank in half of these

■ Otter

saw only six and one of them came and sniffed his boots.

The returning otter appears to be outcompeting and preying on mink, which escaped from fur farms and began breeding in the wild in the 1950s. As well as fish, mink eat chickens, pheasants and the native water vole which has been sent into rapid decline. But the survey found that where otter densities have grown

squares examined during each. In the first survey otter spraints were found at just six per cent of sites. That rose to nearly 10 per cent in the second, and 23 per cent in the latest survey. In the 1970s no otter signs whatsoever were found in 11 of the 32 large squares but now they are present in every one. Britain is the only Western European nation where otters are making a strong recovery.

But the Vincent Trust's report points out that in the Midlands, central-southern and south eastern England otter numbers are still very low, running into dozens rather than hundreds. The total UK population is estimated at about 7,500, with up to1,000 of those living on Shetland where they feed in the sea as well as in rivers. As a top carnivore with a restricted habitat Britain's otter population probably never amounted to more than a few tens of thousands. Its decline began in earnest in the 1830s with the invention of the gin trap and more efficient rifles and the growth of gamekeeping on wealthy estates. There was a short-lived otter recovery during the Great War when the gamekeepers went off to the trenches. But then otter hunting with hounds became popular; during one interwar year 434 were killed for sport in England and Wales. The final, most rapid decline began in the 1950s with the widespread use of dieldrin and aldrin, pesticides used to coat cereal seeds and in sheep dips. These either killed the otters or rendered them infertile. Although this was known by the early 1960s the Ministry of Agriculture did not ban these chemicals in sheep dips until 1966 and a much wider ban on their use did not come in for another 15 years. The otter only gained protection from hunting in 1978. Recovery began as soon as the persecution and poisoning ended, with the otter moving into the deserted areas from its strongholds in the West Country, Wales and Scotland. Radio-tracking has shown that males can move up to 16 kilometres in one night.

The Vincent Trust survey report says the deliberate release of 80 captive-bred otters into the wild in East Anglia, southern England and North Yorkshire has played an important part in re-establishing the animal in these areas. They have bred in the wild for at least two generations. But these releases have been controversial, with some biologists claiming that local rivers and their fish still contained lethally high levels of toxic chemicals, especially the long lasting polychlorinated biphenyls once widely used in making electrical transformers and capacitators. "We know these chemicals are still there and that they do move up the food chain to concentrate in otters," says Dr Don Jefferies, a former Government wildlife scientist who co-authored the 222 page report. "But they seem able to cope. In the South West they're only absent from the most seriously polluted rivers with no fish."

Despite its recovery, the fact that otter numbers are still depressed and the mammal's sheer charisma have won it a place on the list of 116 British plant and animal species for which rescue plans have been proposed. The objective of the otter plan is to restore breeding otters to all the places where they were found in 1960 by the year 2010. That will be achieved by addressing the key present day threats to otters. These are river pollution, a resulting lack of fish, poor bankside cover making it harder for them to find shelter and breed, being run-over on roads and drowned in eel traps. The cost of implementing the otter plan is put at £105,000 a year.

HARBOUR PORPOISE
Phocoena phocoena

The harbour porpoise is the smallest and by far the most common of the whales and dolphins living in the waters around Britain. But its population is thought to be in decline and it is now rarely seen in the English Channel or the southern sector of the North Sea. The best-documented threat it faces is from bottom-set drift nets which are positioned rather like a fine curtain several miles across running along the sea-bed. They are left in place for several days at a time by fishermen seeking to catch flatfish and other high value species which swim near the sea bed. The porpoises become entangled in these nets and drown; surveys have suggested about 10,000 die this way each year, mostly in the North Sea, off the coast of Denmark, and the Celtic Shelf waters off south-west England and southern Ireland.

Scientists believe the porpoise is also vulnerable to long lasting, toxic pollutants which flow down rivers into the sea, get into the small fish it preys upon and then accumulate in the porpoise's ample body fat which forms an insulating blubber layer just under the skin. It may also be

Consequently, little is known about the porpoise's social and family life. It surfaces only briefly to breathe. Earlier this year it emerged that dolphins sometimes kill their smaller relatives in British waters, ramming and battering them. In 1994, Britain's Sea Mammal Research Unit in Cambridge organised a large survey of cetaceans in the North Sea, the English Channel and Celtic Shelf, using ships and aircraft and funded by the European Commission. This led to the first population estimate for the porpoise - between 267,000 and 465,000 dwell in these seas.

The action plan calls for the present population to be maintained, and for ensuring that in the long term no man-made fac-

■ Porpoise

Photography: Dr Ben Wilson/University of Aberdeen

frightened away from busy areas by the noise and movements of ships and boats. The males grow up to 1.7m long. The females are sexually mature at only 14-months-old and they give birth to single calves. They are shy and secretive compared to dolphins, which are often bold, curious and playful with people and ships.

tors stop the porpoise returning to waters where it was formerly found. Among the recommendations for achieving this are further river and coastal pollution curbs, and changes in fishing practices and net design to reduce the drownings. The cost is estimated at £250,000 a year.

RED SQUIRREL
Scirius vulgaris

If it was down to the public, the red squirrel would probably head the list of 116 British plant and animal species for which rescue plans have been proposed. None of our threatened or declining species has won quite so much pity and affection. Its extinction clock started ticking when the much larger, more flexible grey squirrel was introduced here from North America in the late 19th century. Once greys have arrived in an area the reds vanish about 15 years later.

The price tag for implementing the proposed rescue plan for red squirrel is put at £220,000 a year, making it among the most expensive creatures to salvage on the list of 116. The Government is being asked to share the bill with sponsors and

adapted to Britain's wet, deciduous and highly fragmented woodlands than reds. The greys can live at higher population densities and are much more capable of moving across the open country between woods. They are also better at digesting one of the most important available food items, acorns, and they breed faster too.

The reds, whose optimal habitat is the drier coniferous forests of the continent, have found themselves heavily outcompeted and short of food. To add to their struggles, they also seem to suffer from lethal outbreaks of a viral disease called parapox. They are expected to vanish from all but a few patches of England soon into the next century, and from

■ Red Squirrel

Photography: David Black/WWF

charities. There are about 160,000 red squirrels left, mostly in Scotland, while the number of greys has climbed to 2.5 million. They are, it seems, much better

Wales thereafter, unless new and effective ways of controlling the grey squirrels are brought in. Only in the Scots Pine forests north of the border is there a good chance of them meeting the competition once the greys arrive there. The species is also still widespread in Northern Ireland.

The red squirrel can have two broods in one summer if the weather is kind, with three young usually being born in a litter. The species is a keen and competent house builder, making a spherical, roofed nest lined with soft material about one foot across. These dreys (each adult usually has several) are used throughout the year to sleep in as well as for sheltering the babies.

One hope for the future is a small, ingenious food hopper containing grain which only the greys can enter - and then eat poisoned bait. It operates using a balance, and the reds - which are only half the weight of the invading species - are too light to tip it. The grain within is laced with warfarin, a powerful rodent-killer. In 1996 the Government's Forestry Commission was giving this new hopper design a large-scale trial on the Welsh island of Anglesey, where the greys have only recently arrived and the existing red squirrel population is urgently in need of help. Techniques for managing and growing woodlands in ways which favours the reds over the greys are also being investigated. One proposed measure in the action plan is to create 2,000 hectares (eight square miles) of coniferous forest reserves in Wales.

SAND LIZARD
Lacerta agilis

The sand lizard takes its name from the habitat it must have to survive. In midsummer females dig a shallow burrow in a patch of open, sunny sand and lay about eight eggs in it which hatch six weeks later. The young lizards tend to disperse from the nest fairly soon, because if one of the eight inch long adults encounters a juvenile there is a reasonable chance it will be eaten. The lizards hibernate underground in winter, emerging in March of April. It seems that a mild winter does not suit them because it makes them awake too early, leaving them vulnerable to a cold snap.

Once widespread among lowland heaths and coastal dunes they are now down to about 6,000 breeding adults scattered among more than a hundred colonies. Most are in the remaining Dorset and Surrey heathlands, with a few found in sand dunes on Merseyside. Their numbers have plunged across northern Europe. Like nearly all endangered British species of plants and animals, the main reason for their plight is the decline and fragmentation of their habitat. As well as patches of open sand, they need clumpy vegetation a little higher than grazed grass. This gives them the mix of sunshine, shade and cover they require as they scurry around in search of insects, slugs, snails and berries. Being cold blooded, they warm up by basking in sunshine then dash into the shade to avoid overheating. Most of the lowland heaths which provided rough grazing for centuries have become fields, housing or forestry plantations. Much of what remains is being invaded by scrub and bracken. If the heath is not disturbed by man the lizard's essential patches of open sand disappear as vegetation encroaches. But they can make a strong come-back if their habitat is conserved. In 1994 a three year species recovery programme was launched, led by the Herpetological Conservation Trust. Sand lizards have been reintroduced to Welsh sand dunes

■ Sand Lizard

Photography: Hugh Clark/WWF

(they had become extinct in the principality) and sites in Cornwall, Devon and Dorset.

Now the Biodiversity Steering Group's rescue plan says the reptile should be re-established in ten of its former haunts by 2000. Where it still occurs naturally fur-

ther declines must be halted. Most of the plan's recommendations for achieving this concern managing and creating the right habitat. One proposal is to cut down some tree plantations on heathland to link fragments of sand lizard country together. The programme is costed at £80,000 a year.

SCOTTISH CROSSBILL
Loxia scotica

The rare Scottish crossbill may be the only bird unique to British shores. It is thought to be a species which evolved and exists solely in these islands. The Royal Society for the Protection of Birds (RSPB) is funding research to find out if this is case. One of the world's foremost crossbill experts, Dr Jeff Grogh at the American Museum of Natural History in New York, is studying samples of its DNA genetic material and its calls to find out if it is a separate species to

the similar-looking common and parrot crossbills. These are continental species also found in Britain - frequently in the case of the common but much more rarely with the parrot. Dr Grogh should pronounce judgement sometime in 1997. If he decides there is no such thing as the Scottish crossbill thousands of "twitchers" will be plunged into gloom. These keen ornithologists will have to cross the Scottish crossbill off their lists of species they have spotted.

Like the common crossbill, the Scottish bird takes its name from its unusual curved beak with crossed over tips which is specially developed to extract seeds from unripe pine cones. It feeds on Scots pine and only fragments of its haunts, the ancient Caledonian pine forests which once covered much of Scotland, remain. There are estimated to be 1,500 adults in Britain.

The crossbill family all have large heads because of the muscles that

for a bird living in Britain's chilly north, and the young, which are also fed on pine seeds, are fledged in April. The red grouse is another bird species once considered unique to Britain, but it has since been found to be a sub-species of the willow grouse found in Scandinavia. "The Scottish crossbill is our last hope for a bird of our own," says the RSPB.

The rescue plan calls for the protection, creation and management of native pinewoods, and for the moni-

■ Scottish Crossbill   Photography: M.W. Richards/RSPB

power the birds' strong jaws, and the Scottish crossbill has even been known to use its beak to swing from twig to twig. Other birds feed on the open, ripe pine cones in summer but the crossbill is able to snip off unripe ones in winter, break into them while holding on its perch with one foot, then extract the edible parts of the seed. They nest in March, unusually early

toring of sites frequented by Scottish crossbills while the work to clarify whether the bird is unique continues. At the very least, the current British range and population should be maintained. The maximum cost of implementing the action plan for this species is put at £40,000 a year.

SKYLARK
Alauda arvensis

In terms of sheer numbers lost, no British bird has suffered more than the skylark. In the last quarter century the number of breeding birds fell by 1.6 million, roughly halving the UK population. Similar declines have hit this bird of open country across much of Europe. It is thought to have evolved in the Russian steppes, then prospered in Western Europe because the traditional, varied farmscape of meadows and arable fields provided food through the year. In their very best habitat, such

the way in which the male stakes territory and attracts a mate by hovering high and pouring out its long song. If you had to choose one sound to stand for the open countryside this would be it. People have always taken the noise to signify sheer exuberance, "larking about", and the small bird has inspired poetry for centuries. But our ancestors also ate huge quantities of skylarks, and kept them caged and blinded for their song.

■ Skylark

Photography: Mark Hamblin/RSPB

as chalk downland and coastal dunes, up to 75 pairs can be found in a square kilometre. But farming and farmland have changed enormously in the past few decades and the ground nesting skylark cannot survive at anything near their former high density on intensively farmed crop fields.

For now, the species is still common and widespread, instantly recognisable from

The action plan calls for the skylark's population slump in the intensively farmed lowland areas - where it has suffered most harm - to be reversed. Here, the big switch from spring to autumn sown cereals has erased an important winter feeding ground; the stubble fields with their spilt grain. The springtime ploughing and sowing, now largely vanished, was probably also an important food source for the birds. It brought insect larvae and other small creatures to the surface, and afterwards the tiny grain seedlings growing up were also eaten. Skylarks usually fail to breed on fields of autumn sown cereals, but the birds themselves don't seem to realise this. In the early spring the males often start singing above such fields and succeed in attracting females but the the pairs do not go on to make a nest and raise young.

Grasslands were also an important skylark habitat but a large proportion of these has been converted to crop-growing fields and much of the remainder is managed in an intensive way that excludes skylarks. Early cuts of silage grass in May destroy their eggs and chicks, or leave them open to predators.

The skylark was thrown a lifeline in 1992, in the form of the major reform of the Common Agricultural Policy which brought in mass set-aside of arable land. Millions of hectares of crop fields were taken out of production in Britain, leaving weeds and grasses free to grow - which in turn has provided seed and insect food for the skylarks. There are now the first signs that the population decline has slowed. But set-aside may itself disappear within a few years. The conditions which led to its creation - huge crop surpluses and low international grain prices - have entirely disappeared.

The rescue plan calls for more research to establish exactly why the skylark copes so poorly with intensive modern agriculture, and "to consider" altering farming practices and subsidies once the lessons have been learnt. It is costed at up to £104,000 a year.

SONG THRUSH
Turdus philomelos

The song thrush is one of Britain's most common birds, with well over a million breeding here. So why is it on a danger list of 116 plant and animal species for which the Government and conservation groups have proposed rescue plans? For one thing, it has been in rapid decline for at least the last 20 years. For another, it is also one of the best loved really common birds with its handsome colouration and attractive, elaborate song. It is usual for one thrush to have more than 100 different song phrases. Over the past 20 years its numbers in woodland areas have fallen by half, and by almost three quarters in farmland.

There's no shortage of hypotheses for why this should be but not much in the way of established facts. Huge changes in farming are implicated. The wholesale switch from spring to autumn sowing of cereal crops may have deprived the song thrush of an important food source in spring, when the ploughing brought the small, invertebrate animals it eats to the surface. Growing use of molluscicides - pesticides which kill slugs and snails - may have curbed its food supply. The shrinking length of hedgerows may have reduced nesting and feeding areas. Some thrushes migrate from France to Britain to breed here, and it may be that French huntsmen are shooting large numbers of these. Magpies are known to eat the song thrushes' eggs and young chicks (and so are cats) but whether they are partly to blame is far from being proven. Long term monitoring by the British Trust for Ornithology suggest that thrushes are generally hatching out as many chicks as ever, but the survival of the young birds through their first summer and winter has fallen sharply.

The rescue plan has the objective of halting the decline in song thrush numbers by 2000. But it is rather vague about how this can be acheived because the causes are not understood. One proposal is to press for the European Union to ban trying to keep tabs on the life history of each chick that hatches. One interesting early finding from this research is that the Essex birds are failing to raise second broods over the summer, unlike their

■ Song Thrush

Photography: Lawry Hawkey/WWF

French hunters from shooting them. The plan says that much research is needed into how the bird feeds, moves around and rears its young. The Royal Society for the Protection of Birds is carrying out a detailed three year study, looking at one area in the Sussex Downs where the bird is holding its own and another in Essex where there has been a marked decline. A small team of researchers is identifying every thrush territory and every nest site, Sussex cousins. (In a really excellent environment with plenty of food and warmth a pair can raise three broods of chicks in a summer). Another finding; far more thrush 'anvils' surrounded by smashed snail shells occur in Sussex. The anvils are stones which the birds use to break the snails open. The cost of the rescue plan, including this research, is put at up to £124,000 a year.

STAG BEETLE
Lucanus cervus

On a midsummer evening in the south London suburbs a large black speck can sometimes be seen waltzing erratically through the air at rooftop height. It is much too big to be an insect, too small and slow to be a bat or bird.

But it is an insect; Britain's second

largest. This is the huge stag beetle, which is about the same size and weight as Britain's smallest mammal, the pygmy shrew. The males carry huge mandible (jaw) extensions from their mouths which vaguely resemble the antlers of stags. They are often over two inches long and the largest found in Britain was just over three inches. The females are large, too, but lack the formidable mandibles. For unknown reasons, the insect's stronghold is south London and it is also still widespread in the Thames valley, north Essex, south Hampshire and West Sussex. But it is in decline in Britain and the rest of Europe.

Its first three or four years of life are spent

one is levered out of the way. Despite their fearsome appearance, they are incapable of harming people. Yet all too often the reaction of urban man on finding one is to stamp or smash it to death, which may be a factor in its decline.

A more important reason is the removal of dead wood as parks and copses are tidied up. Rotting elm was one of its favourite foods, and the supply of that is now falling fast following the great epidemic of Dutch Elm Disease 25 years ago. The rescue plan's objectives are to identify the beetle's key sites, maintain its population at these sites and find out exactly what its habitat requirements are. Local councils and landowners with parks and

■ Stag Beetle.

Photography: Hugh Clark/WWF

as a larva, munching its way through large pieces of decaying, deciduous wood - often in roots and stumps. Then it turns into a pupa and metamorphosises into the adult. These fly around in search of a mate and they only live for a few weeks. Two males will fight for a female, locking their giant mandibles and wrestling until

woodland must be encouraged to leave decaying stumps in which the larvae can live. The implementation costs are put at £10,000 a year. (Incidentally, Britain's biggest insect is the aquatic great silver water beetle.)

STAR FRUIT
Damasonium alisma

A century ago, Britain was still dotted with tens of thousands of small ponds on commons, village greens and roadsides for farm animals to drink from. Their heavily trampled banks were muddy and the water level rose and fell with the rainfall. At the end of summer there were large areas of dried out mud.

The starfruit is well adapted for coping with the difficult conditions that life on

then re-wetted, but if this does not happen the seeds can remain dormant and viable for decades. So while the annual plant dies out at the end of summer the specialised seeds can restart the cycle of life when the autumn rains flood the dried out mud banks. Cattle helped move the seeds from habitat to habitat on their hooves. Most of these ponds have disappeared now, filled with sediment, trees and scrub because they were no longer

■ Star Fruit.

Photography: © P. Wakely/English Nature

the edge of these ponds presents to water plants. It produces large seeds which either sink to the bottom or float, usually to the water's edge. These only germinate after they have been in dried-out mud

needed. Once fairly common as far north as Yorkshire, the starfruit was restricted to just three ponds by 1990, one in Surrey and two in Buckinghamshire. It gets its name because its small white flowers turn into green fruits which resemble six-pointed stars, each point bearing two seeds. It is no relation to the exotic fruit import found in your local superstore. The plant has already been returned to several of its old ponds by the conservation charity Plantlife, either through restoration work which has reawakened long dormant seeds or by importing the plant.

There was jubilation in Gerrard's Cross, Buckinghamshire in the summer of '96,when volunteers found their muddy struggle to clear out the large New Pond had finally born fruit. Their work in this semi-urban site began in 1992 with a large excavator digging out tonnes of silt. Several large trees which overhung the water were also cut down and scrub removed in an effort to recreate the right

conditions for the plant, last seen there in the mid-1960s. Nothing happened, however, until last year when the dry summer made the pond's water level drop down low. That, in turn, allowed the hidden, long dormant seeds in the sun-baked mud to germinate once levels rose again and in 1996 the starfruit was back and flowering.

The action plan for this species says it should be returned to at least 10 of its old sites by 2004. It suggests all of its known sites today should become government designated Sites of Special Scientific Interest, which would give them some measure of protection from development and damage. The rescue plan, which is centred on ensuring a few ponds are managed in a way which favours this rare and unusual plant, has been costed at £4,000.

STARRY BRECK-LICHEN
Buellia asterella

You could easily overlook this little combination of algae and fungus. It only grows up to one centimetre across as a small, white rosette down on the ground and it is extremely rare. In Britain it is found in small numbers at just a few sites in the Brecklands of Suffolk. This is one of Britain's most unusual habitats, the nearest thing we have to a desert. It has its own climate, more akin to that of central Europe than England. Winters are colder, summers hotter and drier although frosts can occur in almost any month of the year. The Brecklands have thin, sandy, infertile soils overlying chalk and once had large areas of bare ground. The chief reason for this was rabbits, which for centuries were farmed in vast warrens there for their fur and meat. Their endless eating and burrowing kept the vegetation short and large areas of sand exposed. Shifting agriculture was also practised, ploughing land and using it for crops for a

few years before abandoning it as fertility dwindled. The word breck means abandoned field.

This was an abused land - yet it was the abuse that gave it a unique assembly of plant and animal species, including the stone curlew and several rare lichens. At the beginning of this century there were 29,000 hectares of heathland and dry grassland in the Brecklands. Today less than a quarter remains. Since the Twenties the Forestry Commission's huge Thetford forest has grown up in the centre. From the outside intensive arable farming has thrust in, made viable by chemical fertilisers. Pine and birch trees and gorse are encroaching naturally. Air pollution puts nitrate and ammonia in the rainfall which acts as a fertiliser, encouraging rapid grass growth which crowds out the characteristic plant species.

■ Starry Breck-Lichen.

Photography: Peter Lambley

The starry breck lichen is only found on bare patches of sun-baked, chalky earth amid broken turf. The ground does not necessarily have to have been broken up by rabbits; one of its sites at Lakenheath is an old mustard gas dump! Like several of Britain's most threatened plant species, it appears to be an extremely poor competitor which is adapted for exploiting relatively new habitats. The main reasons for its decline are thought to be a lack of rabbit grazing and encroachment by scrub and conifers.

It may be saved. The Breckland has been designated an Environmentally Sensitive Area, which means farmers receive payments for managing their land in a way which conserves the habitat. The European Union has also given conservation organisations £250,000 towards rescue and restoration work for the overall habitat. The action plan for the lichen says the remaining population must be safeguarded and, if feasible, it should be re-introduced to four of its former sites. The programmes of advice to landowners, surveying and research needed to achieve this are costed at £3,000 a year.

STONE CURLEW
Burhinus oedicnemus

The stone curlew is a strange bird. It is a long legged wader which cannot stand the wet. It hunts insects and earthworms at night with its large yellow eyes. It is also one of Britain's most endangered species with only 166 pairs known to have bred here in 1995. The global population runs into the tens of thousands but it is in decline across Europe. A distant relative of the far more common curlew, the stone curlew arrives in April from its winter homes in north Africa and Spain and begins its journey back in September. Today almost all the British birds are found on or around Salisbury Plain or the Breckland, a big sandy area of heath, gorse and grass which straddles the Norfolk Suffolk border. It lays two eggs on chalky, stony or sandy soil. Ground nesting in open country makes the incubating parents, eggs and chicks highly vulnerable to foxes but the jackdaw-sized bird has an effective streaky brown camouflage and a habit of keeping very still.

They can only breed successfully on bare earth or grass cropped short by livestock or

Tractors hoeing and spraying the weeds between the crops put the birds in extreme danger. The Royal Society for the Protection of Birds and English Nature have stone curlew-watchers who place warning markers near dozens of nest sites. Farmers are compensated for keeping away.

The British breeding population has fallen by 85 per cent in the last 50 years. Changes in farming are thought to be the main causes. Most of the pastures where it once fed and nested have been converted to arable fields while much of the remaining grassland now grows too tall in the absence of

■ Stone Curlew.

Photography: Micky White/WWF

rabbits. Tall vegetation is too cool and damp for the warmth-loving chicks and their insect food. The high temperatures and dryness of 1995 are probably why breeding numbers rose by 11 per cent compared to the year before.

About a third breed on Ministry of Defence training grounds but most stone curlews now nest in fields between rows of spring-sown crops such as sugar beet and barley.

livestock grazing. The rescue plan aims is to double the number of breeding pairs in Britain by 2010. This can be done by giving farmers better incentives to manage land in a way which favours the stone curlew and asking the army to do the same on its training grounds. The plan also urges the European Commission to limit or ban the hunting of stone curlews elsewhere in Europe. The cost of implementing the entire stone curlew rescue project is put at £105,000 a year.

VENDACE
Coregonus albula

The vendace is probably the rarest and most threatened freshwater fish in Britain. It has only ever been found in four locations and now it is confined to two Cumbrian lakes, Bassenthwaite and Derwent Water. So what happened to this silver, streamlined fish, once so abundant in its Scottish sites of Mill Loch and Castle Loch in Dumfries and Galloway that clubs were formed to fish for it, that it could have become the

Safeguarding the vendace's remaining natural habitats in Cumbria is the species' best chance of survival. The British Isles offers only a few sites capable of meeting the fish's need for relatively cool and oxygen-rich water, so English Nature is concentrating its efforts on the maintenance of the two suitably deep lakes with clean inshore areas for spawning. Bassenthwaite Lake is a National Nature Reserve owned by

■ Vendace.

Photography: Institute of Freshwater Ecology

only vertebrate known to have been lost from Scotland in the second part of this century?

The species disappeared from Castle Loch after this water body was used to take the town's sewage effluent in 1911. It had expired in Mill Loch by the 1970s due to gradual nutrient enrichment (eutrophication) of the loch and a resulting increase in numbers of coarse fish which preyed upon the eggs and young of the vendace.

the National Trust, so the fish ought to be safe there. The local water company is fitting phosphate-stripping equipment at the small sewage works serving the lakeside town of Keswick, which will reduce the risks of eutrophication.

The action plan calls for a self-sustaining population to be re-introduced in one of the Scottish lochs by 2005, followed by a second reintroduction "if the first is successful and cost-effective." Scottish

Natural Heritage is looking into this. The costs of implementing the action plan are put at a maximum of £32,000 a year.

Vendace typically live for up to six years, by which time they may have grown to up to 28 cms long, and they feed on tiny acquatic invertebrates known as zooplankton. The species is widespread in northern Europe, espe-cially in Scandinavian nations where there are large commercial fisheries. The fact that the remaining British ven-dace have never been heavily exploited by fishermen means they are of consid-erable conservation value. Unlike their continental cousins, they may be the way vendace were before people began to catch large numbers of them - a process which makes fish evolve in new directions.

WATER VOLE
Arvicola terrestris

The water vole - Ratty in Kenneth Grahame's 'The Wind in the Willows' - is still a common little mammal with a UK population of about 1.2 million but its range and population here are both in rapid decline. Larger than that favourite food of kestrels and country cats, the field vole, the water vole is a fine swimmer even though it lacks basic aquatic adapta-tions such as webbed feet and waterproof fur. It eats leaves, stems and roots above and below the water and lives for up to three years. Strangely, this species is capa-ble of a totally terrestrial life away from the riverbank. On the continent its bur-rows are found in the middle of fields, but not in Britain.

A national survey in 1989-90 failed to find signs of the vole at 67 per cent of river-side sites where they were previously recorded. The action plan for this species

Water Vole.

Photography: J. Plant/WWF

says the population decline should be halted now, and by 2010 the species should be allowed to spread back to its 1970 range. Its habitat along canals and rivers is being damaged by erosion from boats and erosion repair work which heaps mounds of river-bed mud on the bankside, sealing its burrows and entombing the vole. Waterside development and the heavy human disturbance which comes from increased river recreation make life uncomfortable or impossible for the vole. Pollution of streams by pesticides used to control rats (rodenticides) may be another cause of decline. But it appears to be the mink, imported from North America for fur farming but now breeding successfully in the wild, which is the last straw for the water vole. It is a voracious predator of small mammals.

The prescription for recovery involves managing rivers, banks and the land nearby in a way which aids the water vole and curbing the use of pesticides.

Anyone who uses rodenticides illegally near where the voles are found should be prosecuted, says the action plan. Mink populations could be controlled by trapping in areas where voles live or to which they might return, although further research is needed to show whether this would be effective. The total cost of the programme is put at £150,000 a year.

The recovery of the otter which is now underway in England gives hope for the vole because it looks as if otters and mink cannot coexist. The larger, native carnivore either kills or chases away the smaller import and this may give the voles a chance. It is too early to know whether this is happening. But given a chance to make a comeback, "ratty" should build his numbers rapidly, for the species is an explosive breeder. Water voles can have five or six litters a year, with six young being born in an underground nest.

YOUNG'S HELLEBORINE ORCHID
Epipactis youngiana

Young's helleborine is an undistinguished-looking orchid but it is very rare, unusual and in need of help. It is only found in Britain. The total population is believed to number less than 1,000 plants, scattered among only a handful of sites. Its habitat is tree-covered spoil heaps found beside old mineral workings. In evolutionary terms it is brand new - a novel plant species which arose as recently as a few decades ago. Botanists believe it may have begun as a hybrid between two closely related orchids.

Like all of its kind, Young's helleborine relies on a fungus entwined in its roots to break down organic matter in the soil and provide nutrition. But while

many orchids have flowers with clever and complex ways of attracting insects then sticking pollen on them, the greeny-white flowers of young's helleborine are self-pollinating. It puts them out, only briefly, in July.

The greatest threat it faces is the bulldozing of the spoil heaps, or bings as they are called in Scotland, which it lives on - either because they are regarded as eyesores which discourage development or because their contents, once waste, are now useful. One site in England was destroyed ten years ago. Bardykes Bing, an old heap on the edge of Glasgow, now holds the biggest known Young's Helleborine population with several hundred plants but the

■ Young's Helleborine Orchid.

Photography: Sidney J. Clark

orchid may have no future there, for a company has been granted planning permission to dig out the entire tip. It uses the red minerals inside for clay tennis courts. Fortunately, this company is sympathetic. It is giving the plant conservation charity Plantlife and the Scottish Wildlife Trust a three year stay of execution. The conservationists hope that the site may yet be safeguarded from destruction or, failing that, the orchids can be transplanted to another bing. Scottish Natural Heritage, the Government's wildlife conservation arm north of the border, also identified Young's Helleborine growing on another threatened bing in central Scotland recently and persuaded the local council, which wanted to remove the spoil tip for development, to desist.

The rescue plan for the orchid includes finding out whether there are any suitable bings to which plants at threatened sites like Bardykes could be transplanted. The implementation costs are put at just £3,000 a year.

Chapter Six

FOUR HABITATS

SALINE LAGOONS

Dotted along Britain's coastline are hundreds of brackish ponds and lakes where saltwater from the sea mixes with freshwater from land. They are called saline lagoons. The words conjure pleasing images of warm, launguid waters but, with British weather and their surroundings of sea walls, shingle, scrubby pastures and housing there is nothing and animal species found in Britain which are adapted to these difficult conditions including insects, worms, molluscs and shrimps and two small species of sea anemone which are found nowhere else. One of these, Ivell's sea anemone, has only ever been found at one place in the world - a small, urbanised lagoon at Shoreham in West Sussex. It was discov-

■ Saline Lagoon

Photography: Glyn Griffiths

remotely azure or tropical about them. For biologists, however, their sometimes murky waters and silty bottoms are one of the most unusual and threatened types of habitat in Britain and Europe. The salt concentrations in their water can vary widely. Gales and high tides can push seawater in raising the salinity, then heavy rainfall can dilute it back down to near freshwater levels. There are some 40 plant

ered there in the 1973, found again ten years later but recent surveys have failed to uncover it; Ivell's may have gone extinct.

Britain has about 300 lagoons which cover only 13 square kilometres. By far the largest is the Fleet, behind the long shingle bank of Dorset's Chesil Beach. In the natural state, new lagoons are constantly being formed. Meanwhile old ones are continuously being lost - either disappearing under the invading sea or becoming gradually less salty, filling up with reeds and sediment and turning slowly into dry land in places where the seashore is extending outwards. But along today's heavily managed coastline a combination of sea walls and development gives new lagoons little chance of forming, while some existing ones have disappeared under buildings and car parks. Other threats are pollution by farm fertilisers, drainage works which affect the freshwater-saltwater balance and the rise in sea level caused by the very slow subsidance of the south eastern part of the British Isles.

The Solent coastline in Hampshire has Britain's biggest concentration of saline lagoons, thanks mainly to the long defunct salt industry. This created a mass of shallow ponds, salterns, in which evaporation turned seawater into concentrated brine. Hampshire County Council has purchased miles of this shore to protect it from development. The council has increased the lagoon area by digging out some ground behind the sea wall and flooding the depression with saltwater.

The Biodiversity Steering Group's action plan calls for at least a square kilometre of new saline lagoon to be created over the next 20 years, for this would only be enough to keep pace with projected losses. It advocates scaling up conservation measures of the kind happening in Hampshire to national level, which would cost about £1.5m a year.

ANCIENT OR SPECIES RICH HEDGEROWS

Hedgerows are uniquely dominant in Britain's countryside - no other country has such a density of them. They provide essential shelter and food for a rich variety of wildlife through the seasons and some are more than 1,000 years old. Yet between 1984 and 1990 nearly a quarter of their total length was lost. The latest Government estimate, from the early 1990s, is that the steady decline continued with more than 10,000 miles a year disappearing due to neglect and deliberate destruction. Little more than ten years ago there were still Government grants available for removing them, in the interests of farm efficiency.

There are about 120,000 miles of the UK's hedgerows which, say the experts, are especially worth saving because of their ecological value and their age. The remainder, about 60 per cent of the total, are mostly less than 200 years old, thinner, and composed largely of hawthorns. These young 'uns date from the great rearrangement of land holdings, the Parliamentary Enclosures, which took place in the 18th and 19th centuries, or are more recent that that.

The older hedgerows form a crucial refuge for wildlife in the intensively farmed lowlands. The more ancient they are, the more varied are the shrubs and smaller plants within them. Some contain species associated with long established woodland, like the wild service tree and bluebells, and woodland animals like the dormouse. In all more than 600 plant species, 1,500 different insects, 65 birds and 25 mammals have been found to use Britain's 280,000 miles of hedgerows. Among this diverse flora and fauna are 13 species which are either in rapid decline or endangered globally.

Most of the destruction is not due to farmers grubbing them out to enlarge fields for the sake of modern crop growing and livestock handling methods. It is down to neglect, or to trimming the hedges in a way which eventually destroys them. The usual method of keeping them tidy is to use a flail cutter bottom grows into thick wood with large gaps in between through which livestock can pass. The structure no longer works, and it no longer looks like a hedge but a straggling, intermittent line of stunted trees and awkwardly shaped old shrubs. There is little reason for the farmer to keep it any more.

■ Hedgerow: Anglesey

Photography: T.D. Timms/WWF

which lops off the top growth once a year. Often this is done in the autumn, scattering and mincing the fruits and nuts which provide food for birds and animals in winter. The hedge grows back, but only at the top. Most hedgerow shrubs and trees do not put out fresh sprouts lower down, so the shaded hedge

The rescue plan for ancient hedgerows advocates cutting them less frequently - every three years say - and a revival of the neglected art of laying hedges, partially cutting then and then bending down the living wood to keep the structure thick and sprouting near its base. But these traditional hedging methods are labour intensive, which is why they have been abandoned. There are limited government grants to pay for hedge planting and restoration but there are nowhere near enough to offset the current rate of loss. The action plan for this habitat calls for up to £3m a year extra of Government funding for hedgerows by 2010.

There are other reasons for the great hedgerow decline. When crops are planted right up to the edge of the fields the hedge bases get doused in fertiliser and pesticides. These days cattle and sheep are kept at higher densities on the land, so the hedges get grazed more heavily.

New planning regulations, which will not apply in Scotland, should provide limited help. These are expected to compel all landowners to notify their local council before they strip out any hedge. The council will then have 28 days in which to decide whether to refuse permission, on the grounds that the boundary is 'important' - particularly historic or rich in plants and animals. The criteria for what constitutes an important hedge are set out in the regulations; they relate mainly to its age and species richness. Ultimately the survival of Britain's hedgerows depends on how many farmers and landowners care about them. The action plan calls for the loss of ancient and species rich hedgerows to end completely by 2005. By then, it urges, half of them should be under sympathetic management which can keep these ancient, oh-so-British structures living for hundreds more years.

CHALK RIVERS

England is blessed with most of Europe's chalk rivers, with 35 of them flowing through the east and south of the country. Where they have managed to survive in their natural state they provide some of the finest river scenery and wildlife habitat in the land - clear, clear water fed from underground chalk aquifers flowing steadily between banks lined with meadows and trees. Water plants rooted on the bottom wave gently in the mid-stream current where trout and salmon swim. Their relatively even flows and water temperatures (which come from being largely fed from aquifers rather than rainwater run-off), their alkaline water (from the chalk) and the way their uppermost reaches, or winterbournes, can dry up almost entirely in summer distinguish them from other types of river.

Most have suffered some damage and some of them massive harm. The principal cause is the taking of too much water direct from the river or, via boreholes, from the rocks beneath. This is done mainly for the benefit of water companies (and therefore us), for farmers irrigating their crop fields and for fish farms. It lowers the depth and flow, allows sediment to accumulate, pollutants to build up their concentration and together these changes reduce the variety of aquatic plants and animals.

Pollution, particularly from sewage works, has over-enriched the water with plant nutrients in several rivers. This enables dense growths of algae to build up, smothering the 'higher', flowering water plants in a slimy coat. That reduces their numbers and sometimes eliminates them entirely. It appears that phosphates from sewage works and farm fertiliser are particularly important, because it is a lack of this nutrient - rather than the nitrates also used as farm fertiliser - which limits the growth of algae in the natural state. About half of the phosphate in sewage effluent comes from detergents, with the

■ River Test.

Photography: © P. Wakely/English Nature

rest from the food we eat. Intensive farming of the land beside the chalk rivers has also harmed them. The old meadows are now dosed with fertiliser to grow wheat and barley or large quantities of grass. This adds to the quantity of silt and plant nutrients flowing into the river. Finally, long stretches of these rivers have been fundamentally changed by dredging or by being put into concrete-lined culverts.

A damaged river often loses its water crowfoot plants, or has their growth retarded for several months from spring into summer. These plants are among the most characteristic of chalk rivers. They grow up from the stream bottom towards the surface early in the year, forming submerged thickets in which numerous invertebrates live, food for trout and salmon. But the kind of man-made changes discussed above cause an oozy, nutrient-rich sediment to build up on the stream bottom. The water crowfoot puts out only short roots in this insubstantial substrate and as it grows it gets uprooted and swept away by the current.

The action plan for this habitat calls for pollution to be curbed and natural flows restored on the small minority - about 3.5 per cent of the total length - of Britain's chalk rivers which have been or will be officially designated as Sites of Special Scientific Interest. These eight actual or proposed SSSI chalk rivers - the Frome, upper Hull, Itchen, Kennet, Lambourn, upper Nar, Test and the Hampshire Avon - are the jewels in the crown, the most pristine and wildlife-rich. Even so, two thirds are damaged to some extent. Most have elevated phosphate concentrations thanks to 12 sewage works dotted along them

Some restoration work had begun before the plan was written. A very few sewage works have had phosphate stripping equipment fitted. Along three of these rivers there are Government incentives for farmers to manage the land in an environment-friendly way. But, says the plan, much more will have to be done in the way of reducing pollution and the amount of water taken from boreholes, and improving the management of the banks and farmland along the rivers. It calls for other non-SSSI chalk rivers to be restored where this is judged to be affordable. The cost to the Government of safeguarding and improving chalk rivers to the point where 4,000 miles of them are in good condition by 2010 is put at £1m a year.

UPLAND OAKWOODS

Scattered along the high ground of the western edge of Britain, from southern Scotland down to the West Country, are tattered remnants of the great forests which once covered almost the entire country 6,000 years ago. These beautiful broadleaf woodlands of the uplands differ among themselves quite markedly, but they have enough in common to set them apart from the woods of lower altitudes. They are dominated by oak, although the number of birch trees rises in Scotland. They grow slowly, because of the thinner soils and tougher conditions found higher up. And because the air on the western side of the country is usually cleaner, with fresh air blown in from the Atlantic on the prevailing winds, tree trunks and branches are festooned with a variety of grey green lichens, some of them huge and dangling. Most lichens cannot abide much air pollution. The upland oakwoods are found elsewhere along Europe's Atlantic coastline, but not on high ground deeper inside the continent; inland mountains and hills lack the necessary mild climate, humidity and rainfall which comes from being beside an ocean.

One of the strangest and most impressive bits of upland oakwood is Wistman's Wood in the middle of Dartmoor, 1,300 feet up. It only covers a few acres and consists of several clumps of oak scattered along a steep sided stream valley but it has been a favourite place among botanists for a century. The oaks grow among moss-covered boulders. They are old - some of them are more than 200 years, quite small and low and extraordinarily warped and gnarled. The boughs and trunks, which are often horizontal, are absolutely covered in a riot of ferns, mosses and lichens with even the occasional entire bilberry bushes growing on the thin mat of soil which has collected in depressions in the wood. On one square foot of bark you can find three species of moss and three of lichen, and overall there are more than 200 species of moss, lichen and fern found in these woods. All these epiphytes (plants which grow on other plants) and green lushness makes Wistman's look a little like a bonsai rainforest. It certainly gets high rainfall - about 80 inches a year.

Britain and Ireland have most of Europe's upland oakwoods. In the UK they are found in Devon, Cornwall and Cumbria in England, Gwynedd in Wales and Lochaber and Argyll in Scotland. About one third of their total area is thought to have been lost in the past 60 years with

whose dense shade wipes out almost everything living beneath it.

The action plan for this key habitat calls for all of the remaining area to be conserved by applying the right sort of management, for the total area to be increased by 10 per cent on open ground through planting and allowing natural regeneration, and for another 10 per cent of ex-upland oakwood which has been damaged by conifer planting or rhododendron invasion to be restored. The right sort of management usually means doing very

■ Wistman's Wood, an upland oakwood.

Photography: Francis Sullivan/WWF

around 800 square kilometres remaining. The main reasons for this decline were replacement with conifer plantations, clearance for quarrying, and felling for rough grazing by upland sheep and cattle. Today they are rather better protected and valued, with about a quarter of the total area designated as Sites of Special Scientific Interest. But some are still being harmed, chiefly by over-grazing by sheep and deer and invasion by fast-spreading thickets of rhododendron,

little apart from ensuring young oak trees filling in gaps are not all grazed to death by sheep and deer. A little light grazing can, however, stop brambles from becoming too rampant. The costs of safeguarding what remains and bringing in the extra habitat are put at £3.4m in 1997 rising to £11.6m in 2010.

Appendix One

THE OTHER 90 SPECIES

MAMMALS

Brown hare, *Lepus europaeus*.
First imported to Britain by the Romans, the hare has declined rapidly since the Second World War. The reduction in the

■ Brown Hare.   Photograhy: Hugh Clark/WWF

variety of crops on farms and the switch to autumn sown cereals has reduced the hare's food supply. Vast areas of old grasslands, one of its favourite habitats, have gone under the plough, while the meadows which remain are cut much earlier in the summer for silage, when it is giving birth to its leverets. The hare's UK population is thought to be between 600,000 and two million and its decline may now have stabilised due to the advent of the set-aside policy which takes croplands out of production. It can run at 30mph and

weighs three times as much as a rabbit.

Greater horseshoe bat, *Rhinolophus ferrumequinum*.
A insect-eating bat, so called because of its horseshoe shaped nose, which has declined throughout northern Europe this century. In Britain it is now restricted to south west England and south Wales, with only 4,000 to 6,000 remaining. The action plan calls for this to be increased by 25 per cent by 2010.

BIRDS

Aquatic warbler, *Acrocephalus paludicola*.
This small, globally threatened bird passes through southern Britain in autumn during its migration between eastern Europe and Africa. Only a few hundred are thought to use our reedbeds as a staging post but this may be more than a tenth of their entire world population. The action plan calls for the strongest possible protection of reedbeds it is known to use.

Corncrake, *Crex crex*.
The strange, noisy nocturnal calls of the male corncrake - it sounds a little like a football rattle - used to be well-known to country folk before the last war. The corncrake has suffered an extremely rapid decline for more than a century and in Britain this migratory bird is now thought to breed only in the Hebrides and Orkney with about 600 calling males recorded. The reason is the loss of traditional hay meadows where it nested to modern silage making or permanent pasture. Conservation efforts by the Royal

Society for the Protection of Birds, Scottish Natural Heritage and local farmers are now showing some success.

■ Grey Partridge.   Photograhy: Phil Banks/WWF

Grey partridge, *Perdix perdix*.
The UK population of this once extremely common farmland bird halved between 1970 and 1990 to about 150,000 pairs. It is now virtually extinct in Northern Ireland. The grey partridge is a victim of modern agriculture, with the increased use of herbicides and pesticides killing the insect food on which its chicks depend.

Capercaille, *Tetrao urogallus*.
The world's biggest grouse has already become extinct in Scotland once, in the 18th century. It was reintroduced from Europe into its habitat of Scots Pine forests in the middle of the last century but in recent decades it has declined rapidly there and across northern Europe. There are about 2,200 birds in the UK. The causes of its misfortunes are uncer-

tain but flying into the fences which keep out tree-eating red deer is one.

FISH

Allis shad, *Alosa alosa*, and Twaite shad, *Alosa fallax*.
These are two closely related, medium sized sea fish found in shallow waters and estuaries along the coasts of western Europe and parts of the Mediterranean. Both swim into the lower reaches of rivers to spawn. The populations of these two silvery species have fallen due to river pollution, overfishing and the construction of dams and weirs across rivers. The allis may breed in only a few French rivers, while the twaite still spawns in the Wye, Usk, Severn - where it is still fished - and Tywi rivers in Wales, and possibly around some rivers mouths in the Solway Firth on the Scottish border.

Pollan, *Coregonus autumnalis pollan*.
This silvery, medium sized freshwater fish is thought to be unique to Ireland. It is found in Lough Neagh, Northern Ireland, where its numbers are still high enough to support commercial fishing, and in nearby Lower Lough Erne where it is extremely rare. The species is also found in a few loughs and rivers in the Irish Republic. Its populations have fallen because of eutrophication (over-fertilisation) of its lakes by farm fertiliser and sewage, competition with introduced roach and over-fishing.

INSECTS

Butterflies and moths

Large blue butterfly, *Maculinea arion*.
The caterpillars of this grassland species eat the grubs of an ant. It became extinct in Britain in 1979, but was re-introduced

■ Large Blue. Photograhy: © P. Wakely/English Nature

successfully in the 1980s using Swedish butterflies.

Large copper butterfly, *Lycaena dispar.*
Became extinct in Britain in 1851 after its fenland habitat declined, but a Dutch subspecies was reintroduced to Woodwalton Fen in Cambridgeshire in 1927. This was not a great success; to keep the colony going the butterfly had to be re-introduced at this site or its numbers built up using captive-bred stock on several occasions.

■ Heath Fritillary. Photograhy: © P. Wakely/English Nature

Heath fritillary, *Mellicta athalia.*
Now rare and restricted to southern England around three main centres, Exmoor, east Cornwall and Kentish woodland where it breeds on healthland, grassland and newly coppiced woods respectively. Its food plant is common cow-wheat.

Marsh fritillary, *Eurodryas aurinia.*
Britain is a stronghold for this fast declining species, which remains widespread in parts of the West Country and Wales. Its habitat is traditionally managed grasslands and its foodplant is devil's-bit scabius.

Pearl bordered fritillary, *Boloria euphrosyne.*
A rapidly dwindling butterfly of woodland and traditionally-managed grass-

■ Pearl Bordered Fritillary. Photograhy: J. Plant/WWF

lands, it is still widespread and abundant at some locations in Wales, southern and north west England and the Scottish Highlands. Its caterpillars feed on violets.

Silver spotted skipper butterfly, *Hesperia comma.*
Once recorded as far west as Devon and as far north as Yorkshire, it is now con-

fined to short turf on chalk grasslands on the North and South Downs where it breeds on sheep's fescue.

Bright wave moth, *Idaea ochrata.*
Lives along sandy shingle beaches and sand dunes in only three areas in Suffolk, Essex and Kent. Little is known about its ecology.

Speckled footman moth, *Coscinia cribraria.*
Found in large numbers by collectors a century ago, but now restricted to heathlands around Wareham in Dorset with no large colonies known.

Ants

Black-backed meadow ant, *Formica pratensis.*
Widespread but declining in Europe, but in Britain it has only ever been recorded at a few sites in Dorset. No sightings in the UK since the 1980s so it may be extinct here.

Black bog ant, *Formica candida.*
Known from only a few bogs, wet heaths and mossy stream sides in Dorset and Hampshire and an isolated site in Dyfed, Wales. This endangered ant seems to have dwindled particularly in its former stronghold of the New Forest.

Narrow-headed ant, *Formica exsecta.*
A large-jawed, aggresive ant whose queens can infiltrate a neighbouring colony of another ant species and trick their workers into accepting her instead of their own queen. Found in a few areas in Devon, Dorset and Hampshire and in some Scots pine forests north of the border. Thinly scattered across Europe, it is endangered in Britain.

Beetles

A dung beetle, *Aphodius niger.*
This tiny beetle relies completely on cattle dung trodden into the edge of ponds, on which its larvae feed. It has only ever been found at a handful of sites in the New Forest.

Blue ground beetle, *Carabus intricatus.*
A very large, glossy blue beetle which is declining across Europe. Only ever found at a few West Country sites in Britain. This flightless, predatory and extremely elusive beetle loves to eat slugs and can only live in mature oak and beech woods with sparse ground vegetation and high humidity.

A ground beetle, *Bembidion argenteolum.*
Used to be found around Lough Neagh in Northern Ireland but has not been recorded there for over 70 years. Only recent UK records are from Rye, Sussex. Found in northern and central Europe, and in Russia, where it lives on damp, fine sand beside freshwater.

A ground beetle, *Panagaeus crux-major.*
Once widespread in wetlands in Wales and England, this small beetle is now found at only three British sites - flood meadows in the Lower Derwent Valley, Yorkshire and in dunes in Dyfed, Wales and Lincolnshire. It is black with two prominent red spots on its wing cases.

A ground beetle, *Tachys edmondsi.*
Unique to the UK, this beetle has only ever been found living on moss in bogs in Hampshire's New Forest. It has not been seen in 20 years and may be extinct.

Two closely related leaf beetles, *Cryptocephalus coryli* and *Cryptochephalus exiguus.*
Just 40 years ago coryli was widespread in southern England but it is now found only at single sites in Surrey and

Berkshire and on Lincolnshire heaths. It lives on hazel and young birch leaves. Its cousin, exiguus, has only ever been recorded at a few sites in the Norfolk Broads and Lincolnshire fens in the 19th century. Since 1910 it has only been known from one Suffolk fen, Pashford Poors in Suffolk. Two recent surveys have failed to find it there so it may be globally extinct.

A longhorn beetle, *Orbera oculata.*
Since 1890 this half-inch long, black and orange beetle has only been found in a small area of fenland next to Wicken Fen, Cambridgeshire. Its larvae eat willow shoots and it gets its name from its long, horn-like antennae.

A rove beetle, *Stenus palposus.*
This insect is very thinly scattered across Europe, living in fine, damp sand close to large freshwater lakes. Only ever found in Britain from a small area on the shoreline of Lough Neagh, Northern Ireland.

Violet click beetle, *Limoniscus violaceus.*
This half-inch long insect gets its name from the sound it makes when its body suddenly and violently arches, flinging it into the air to escape predators. It is rare throughout Europe and in Britain is found only on Bredon Hill in Worcestershire and in Windsor Forest. It breeds in the hollows of ancient beech and ash trees.

Broad-nosed weevil, *Cathormiocerus britannicus.*
First discovered in Cornwall in 1908, this plant-eating beetle has only ever been found at a few cliff sites on the Lizard Penninsula and a roadside bank in Dorset.

Flies

Hornet robberfly, *Asilus crabroniformis.*
A huge, predatory fly up to one and a half inches long, found on traditionally managed grassland and heath in southern England and Wales. It preys on grasshoppers, dung beetles and other flies. Its habitats have declined and so has the fly.

A hoverfly, *Callicera spinolae.*
A large, metallic-bronze coloured fly rare in western Europe and on the brink of extinction in Britain. Now thought to survive at only one parkland site in Cambridgeshire where it breeds in rot holes in two beech trees. One of these trees was felled in a gale in 1995 but has since been pushed upright.

A hoverfly, *Chrysotoxum octomaculatum.*
A wasp mimic with black and yellow warning bands on its body. Always rare, it has only ever been recorded at places in southern England. Recent sightings have almost all been in Surrey and it is thought to be in rapid decline.

Bee

Shrill carder bee, *Bombus sylvarum.*
Widespread and common in southern England a century ago, but in the 1980s only seven sites where this bumblebee still lingers were found. It needs herb-rich rough grasslands.

Damselfly

Southern damselfly, *Coenagrion mercuriale.*
Threatened through most of its range from Europe to north Africa. This black and blue insect resembling a small dragonfly prefers heathland streams and has declined rapidly in Britain in the last 30 years. Now found in scattered locations across southern England, south Wales and Anglesey.

OTHER INVERTEBRATES.

White clawed crayfish, *Austropotamobius pallipes.*
This four inch long crustacean, a freshwater-dwelling relative of the lobster, has been hard hit by the important and subsequent rapid spread of the much larger, more aggressive North American signal crayfish. This not only appears to outcompete it, but also carries a fungal disease which has proved lethal to the native species.

The little whirlpool ram's-horn snail, *Anisus vorticulus.*
A tiny, very rare water-dwelling snail found in unpolluted, chalky ditches

■ Shining Pond Snail.   Photograhy: © R. S. Key/English Nature

which drain marshes. It has only ever been found at a few sites in East Anglia, Middlesex and Sussex and has not been found outside East Anglia in the last ten years.

Glutinous snail, *Myxas glutinosa.*
This freshwater-dwelling snail has recently been found at just one site near Oxford after years of decline. It is 15mm long and has a very thin-walled, bubble-like shell. It needs clean, crystal clear, 'hard' water with firm stream and river bottoms to crawl along.

Sandbowl snail, *Catinella arenaria.*
A tiny snail with an oval shell recorded at only three sites in Britain, one in a damp sand dune in the West Country and the others near upland calcareous springs in northern England. A relict from the end of the last Ice Age.

Shining pond snail, *Segmentina nitida.*
Has an iridescent shell just 7mm across. Lives in unpolluted, usually chalky waters of the ponds and drains of grazing marshes. It has declined rapidly in Britain this century and is now confined to the Norfolk Broads, the Pevensey Levels in East Sussex and possibly a couple of other nearby sites.

Narrow-mouth whorl snail, *Vertigo angustior,* **Round-mouthed whorl snail,** *Vertigo genesii,* **and another Whorl snail,** *Vertigo geyeri.*
Three rare, tiny and closely related snail species, all of which are found at very restricted number of sites in Europe and only a handful of sites in Britain. Their oval shells are no more than 2.5mm long.

Depressed river mussel, *Pseudanodonta complanata.*
Another freshwater mussel which is now seriously threatened throughout its European range - southern Britain is a stronghold. Threats are thought to include water pollution, damage to river banks, drought and the collection of molluscs for garden ponds and aquaria.

Freshwater pea mussel, *Pisidium tenuilineatum.*

Rare in Britain and throughout Europe, and in decline recently, especially along canals and rivers north of London where it was once found. So called because of its small size.

Freshwater pearl mussel, *Margaritifera margaritifera.*
The larvae of this big, rare and declining river-dwelling mussel live as parasites in the gills of salmon and trout. It grows up to five inches long, can live up to 30 years, and sometimes has pearls inside - which has caused it to be heavily overfished. Recently it has been found in large numbers in a river in Cumbria.

Ivell's sea anemone, *Edwardsia ivelli.*
Extremely rare and possibly now extinct. This small, undistinguished looking species was first identified in 1973 living in a small, saltwater lagoon in Shoreham, West Sussex. It has never been found anywhere else and was last seen there in 1983.

Starlet sea anemone, *Nematostella vectensis.*
This is only found in a few coastal lagoons in the Isle of Wight, Sussex, Hampshire and Dorset and in some brackish ponds and ditches.

FLOWERING PLANTS

Ribbon-leaved water plantain, *Alisma gramineum.*
A freshwater perennial now found only in a shallow lake in Worcestershire and a drainage channel in Lincolnshire. Rare in Europe, too.

Creeping marshwort, *Apium repens.*
A small, creeping plant which grows in damp, winter-flooded pasture. The British population is thought to number only about 100 plants in one Oxfordshire meadow.

Norwegian mugwort, *Artemisia norvegica.*
This globally rare little alpine is found only in Norway, the Ural mountains and three peaks in northern Scotland.

Mountain scurvy-grass, *Cochlearia micacea.*
Another alpine which may be unique to the Britain, found on mountain soils with a high metal content.

Lundy cabbage, *Coincya wrightii.*
A short lived perennial, this cabbage is found growing only on the south eastern

■ Lundy Cabbage.　　　　Photograhy: D. Rostron/WWF

cliffs and slopes of Lundy Island in the Bristol Channel. A beetle species unique to Lundy and this plant lives on it.

Wild cotoneaster, *Cotoneaster cambriscus.*
Possibly unique to Britain, and here found only at a single, secret mountainside site in Wales where it numbers at most a few dozen individuals.

Lady's slipper orchid, *Cypripedium calceolus.*

A large, beautiful orchid growing on limestone grassland. Once found scattered across northern England, it now survives naturally at only one site. A victim of

■ Lady's Slipper.   Photograhy: C. Lister/WWF

more intensive grazing by farm animals and theft by orchid enthusiasts.

Eyebrights, *Euphrasia species.*
A group of rare plants, unique to Britain, found on damp, lowland heaths, seaside heaths and grassland, dune grass and salt marsh.

Western ramping-fumitory, *Fumaria occidentalis.*
Also unique to Britain, this plant of hedgebanks, walls and waste ground is now found only in Cornwall and the Isles of Scilly.

Fen orchid, *Liparis loeselii.*
Recently this orchid has been found at only four sites, two in the Norfolk Broads

and two in South Wales dunes. Also found in Europe, but rare.

Floating water-plantain, *Luronium natans.*
This freshwater plant spread from its natural strongholds in the lakes of Snowdonia and mid-Wales in the last century via the growing canal system. A poor competitor which needs still water, it is rare in Britain and the rest of Europe.

Slender naiad, *Najas flexilis,* and **holly-leaved naiad,** *Najas marina.*
Two closely related and rare freshwater species. The slender naiad prefers deep water and, in the UK, it is now found only in Scotland, mostly in lochs on islands off the west coast. Its cousin is found regularly in only three of the Norfolk Broads.

Shetland pondweed, *Potamogeton rutilus.*
Another rare freshwater plant, found growing on the bottom at least three feet deep. Found in lochs in northern Scotland, the Western Isles and Shetland.

Three-lobed crowfoot, *Ranunculus tripartitus.*
Small, delicate and found in shallow ponds, ditches and ruts which dry out in summer. Found in southern England but rare, with its stronghold on the Lizard peninsula in Cornwall. In decline in northern Europe.

Shore dock, *Rumex rupestris.*
A seaside species found in a few sites in Anglesey, South Devon, Cornwall and the Isles of Scilly, but the largest UK population has less than 50 plants. Declining in the UK and in its European haunts on the Atlantic coastlines of Spain and France.

Yellow marsh saxifrage, *Saxifraga hirculus.*
A small, perennial plant found on boggy,

alkaline soils, it is rare and declining in Britain and across Europe. Its largest concentrations are in the northern Pennines.

FERNS

Newman's lady fern, *Athyrium flexile.*
Found only at a very few high mountain sites in Scotland, this fern may be unique to Britain.

Killarney fern, *Trichomanes speciosum.*
A fern of Atlantic islands including Britain, the asexual form (sporophyte) is extremely rare and found only in a very few widely scattered damp caves and stream ravines. The sexual form is much more widespread.

FUNGI

Sandy stilt puffball, *Battarraea phalloides.*
In Britain, this fungus is only seen regularly at one hedge bank in Suffolk.

Devil's bolete, *Boletus satanas.*
UK population may now be confined to two beech woods on the South Downs.

A fungus, *Tulostoma niveum.*
Grows among moss clumps on limestone boulders, and found at only nine sites in Europe including one near a waterfall in Scotland.

LICHENS

Orange-fruited elm-lichen, *Caloplaca luteoalba.*
Now largely confined to the bark of mature, isolated elms in drier areas. Dutch elm disease, which destroyed almost all mature elms, has done critical damage. Very rare across Europe.

River jelly lichen, *Collema dichotomum.*
A freshwater lichen growing on submerged, partially shaded rocks and boulders in unpolluted, fast-flowing streams. Now very rare in Britain.

Elm's gyalecta, *Gyalecta ulmi.*
Found on calcareous rock outcrops at just six sites in Scotland and one in Northumberland, although it used to be found occasionally on elm trees.

Two closely related lichens, *Pseudocyphellaria aurata* and *Pseudocyphellaria norvegica.*
Aurata is widespread along coastlines in the southern hemisphere but has declined dramatically in Britain and is now found only on the Channel Island of Sark and a single island off the west coast of Ireland. Norvegica is known at only one site in England and a few in Scotland, although it is also found in Ireland, Norway, Madeira, the Azores and Chile. Both species grow on trees and heather.

Schismatomma graphidioides.
Very rare in Britain and Europe, this species is found on the bark of beech, ash and oak in ancient parkland or open woodland. The New Forest is its British stronghold.

MOSSES

Cornish path-moss, *Ditrichum cornubicum.*
A moss only found in Britain and at only one site in Cornwall since 1963, on an old metal mine spoil heap.

Derbyshire feather-moss, *Thamnobryum angustifolium.*
This species is confined to the UK, and found in just one location - a shady lime-

stone rock-face beside a spring in Derbyshire.

Glaucous beard-moss, *Didymodon glaucus.*
Grows in dry crevices on bare chalk and limestone. Rare in Europe and confined, in Britain, to one site in Wiltshire.

Green shield moss, *Buxbaumia viridis.*
Recently found at only one site in Britain, in Scotland. This species grows on decaying conifer wood in sheltered, shady places.

Slender green feather-moss, *Hamatocaulis vernicosus.*
A rare moss living on alkaline wetlands which is extremely difficult to tell apart from a close relative - you have to examine the stems through a microscope to distinguish between them.

Weissia multicapsularis.
A rare, ephemeral moss which grows on damp clay soils. Its UK stronghold is Cornwall where it grows mainly on banks beside tracks and paths.

LIVERWORTS

Atlantic lejeunea, *Lejeunea mandonii.*
In the UK it has been recorded at just one site in Cornwall since 1970. Found along Atlantic coastlines on rocks, trees and rotting logs in shady, sheltered sites.

Marsh earwort, *Jamesoniella undulifolia.*
Found in mineral-rich bogs, but in recent years recorded at just two British sites - in Cornwall and Argyll.

Norfolk flapwort, *Lophozia rutheana.*
Always rare, this liverwort of extremely wet, chalky fens has lately been seen at only one site in Norfolk. Rare and declining in Europe.

Petalwort, *Petalophyllum ralfsii.*
Found in ponds in dunes (dune slacks) dotted around Britain, but rare.

Western rustwort, *Marsupella profunda.*
Globally rare, in Britain it is now found at just one site in disused Cornish china clay workings.

STONEWORTS

Mossy stonewort, *Chara muscosa.*
Only ever identified at a handful of locations in Britain and Ireland, it grows on sand in shallow freshwater. It has not seen since the 1930s so may be extinct.

Appendix Two

THE OTHER TEN HABITATS

Reedbeds

These are wetlands which are flooded for most of the year. They are dominated by the common reed *Phragmites australis.*, and are among the most important the reedbeds but when they are left to themselves scrub and trees usually encroach, then the habitat becomes a boggy wood and dries out. Some reedbeds along England's east coast are threatened by the invading sea - the land is slowly sinking here, and sea levels are expected

■ Reedbeds.

Photography: ©P. Wakely/English Nature

British habitats for rare birds such as the bittern, marsh harrier and crane. Reedbeds also include open water, ditches and small areas of scrubby willow woodland. The UK has about 50 square kilometres of reedbed scattered among some 900 mostly small sites; only about 50 of these cover more than 50 hectares. This habitat has declined drastically mainly because of water boreholes and drainage works which have converted them to farmland. The long established tradition of taking reeds for thatch used to preserve

to rise gradually due to global warming.

The action plan includes identifying and, if necessary, rehabilitating reedbeds which cover more than two hectares and creating 12 square kilometres of new reedbed from land of little wildlife interest (such as intensively farmed cereal fields) by 2010 in blocks of at least 20 hectares. The annual cost is estimated to be between £200,000 and £570,000 in the year 2000.

Cereal Field Edges

The intensive arable farming practised across most of lowland Britain, with crops growing right up to hedges and fences and heavy pesticide and fertiliser use, has done great harm to wild plants

If all the cereal field edges in Britain were managed in a more wildlife-friendly manner that would create an extra 2,000 square kilometres of useful feeding and breeding grounds for hundreds of different insect species, dozens of birds and mammals. That's an area a little larger than greater London. Rare flowers like the

■ Cereal Field Edges.

Photography: P. J. Banks/WWF

and animals. But there are ways of managing a strip of land - up to six metres wide - between the crop and the field edge which turns it into a wildlife refuge. One method is to leave this strip fallow, under grass or last year's stubble. Others are to plant this strip with a cereal crop but use no pesticides there and forsake harvesting it, or to plough it once a year and plant no crop.

corn buttercup, corn parsley and corn gromwell which used to be common in cereal fields 50 years ago would also gain.

Hundreds of hectares of cereal field edges are already managed for the benefit of wildlife, thanks to various incentive schemes run by the Ministry of Agriculture and the Game Conservancy Trust, as well as the goodwill of conservation-minded farmers. The action plan for this habitat proposes expanding this area to 150 square kilometres by 2010. It would cost up to £2.1m a year to achieve this, with the money spent on incentives to farmers.

Fens

The word fen covers a wide variety of peaty boglands and their soils and waters can range from acid to alkaline. Some have been found to have up to 550 species of higher plants, (a third of all the species found in Britain,) and half of our dragon-fly species living on them. Once they covered huge areas of the country but they have been in decline for hundreds of years as drainage turned them into fields; thus the East Anglian fenlands are mostly fens no more. Water boreholes have also dried out many, helping scrub and trees to encroach. The action plan calls for the fens which are most important to wildlife

underway by that year. That means ensuring that the water flowing into them, the lifeblood of fens, is not polluted with fertiliser and sewage, and is available in sufficient quantities. The cost of the plan is put at £70,000 a year by 2000.

Limestone Pavements

Limestone pavement is a rare habitat which cannot be recreated once it disappears. It consists of areas of flat, bare limestone with vegetation clinging to its edges or growing in the many cracks which criss-cross it. The limestone was ground flat by ice sheets in the last Ice Age; during the thousands of years since then running water has widened the cracks in the rock into a complex pattern of crevices. The pavements are found in a few places in Wales, northern England, Northern Ireland and Scotland with the

■ Limestone Pavement.

Photography: Chris Tydeman/WWF

to all be identified by 2005 with rehabilitation of those which have been damaged

largest areas in North Yorkshire and Cumbria. All told, there are less than 25 square kilometres. They are home to a wide variety of flowering plants, ferns and lichens, some of them rare. The ash, yew and thorn trees which struggle to grow in their meagre soil are usually stunted and warped from drought and howling winds, taking decades to grow only a few feet tall.

The greatest threat to the pavements is the removal of the limestone to provide ornamental stone for rockeries. Although local councils can protect pavements by

Lowland Heathland

A beautiful, melancholy landscape of poor, peaty and sandy soils dominated by heather plus the occasional bog, patch of bare ground, scattered trees and scrubs. The lowland heaths have their own, highly characteristic plants and animals and several of these - such as the Dartford warbler and sand lizard - are now very rare. Britain has about 580 square kilometres of this habitat left with most of it in

■ Heathland: Coombeheath

Photography: J. Plant/WWF

designating them under the Wildlife and Countryside Act 1981, illegal quarrying continues. There are also two landowners with planning permission to legally extract the valuable rock, which can fetch over £100 a tonne. The action plan says there should be no further loss of pavement or damage to what little remains, which means ending all use in gardening and landscaping. The cost of implementation include £500,000 to compensate the two landowners who have planning permission to extract their limestone.

England; 200 years ago it had five times as much. Dorset has the largest areas.

Over the years the heathland has been lost to farmland, quarrying and house-building; large areas have disappeared under south coast suburbs. These days the main threats are encroachment by trees and scrub as rough grazing and other traditional uses of the landscape have declined. The action plan for this habitat says all of what remains needs to be maintained and improved and a further 60 square kilometres re-established on former heathlands to link fragments of remaining habitat into larger blocks. The costs of doing this are put at between £800,000 and £4.3m a year by the year 2000.

Coastal and Floodplain Grazing Marsh

Grazing marshes harbour a rich variety of plants, invertebrates and birds. These are flat expanses beside the coast or rivers where farmers have long grazed sheep and cattle or cut grass for hay. After heavy rainfall or extreme high tides the marshes might flood for several weeks but a network of ditches keeps the water level under control and the land usable for most of the year. The ditches never run dry and the water within them has a diverse community of water plants and invertebrates. The grassland also has numerous wildflowers and large numbers of wading birds such as snipe, lapwing and curlew raise their young there in summer. In winter migrating wildfowl including Bewick and whooper swans feed on the marshes. There are estimated to be about 3,000 square kilometres left in Britain although only about 100 square kilometres of this has never been fertilised and remains semi-natural. Fertiliser use can sharply reduce the number of species living on the grass and in the ditches.

Probably about half the total area of grazing marsh has been lost in the past 60 years, although along the Thames estuary the loss is thought to be around two thirds. The main reasons have been flood defence works which have stopped the periodic flooding and dried marshes out, conversion to crop fields or to intensive grass growing for silage and the building of houses or other development. The action plan calls for 100 square kms of grazing marsh which has become too dry or too intensively managed to be rehabilitated by 2000, and for the re-conversion of 25 square kms which has become crop fields. The extra cost to taxpayers - over and above what is already spent on conserving the marshes - is put at £13.2m a year in 2010, roughly a doubling. The money would be spent on subsidies to farmers and on buying intensively farmed land in order to make it revert to grazing marsh.

Purple Moor Grass and Rush Pastures

In Devon they call them the Culm Grasslands. Between 1984 and 1991 nearly half were converted into normal, intensively managed farmland, a staggering rate of loss. These somewhat boggy, livestock grazing areas are found on poorly drained and usually acidic soils in lowland areas with high rainfall. Britain has about 560 square kms left which is a large fraction of all of this semi-natural habitat remaining in Europe. In these islands they are found in the West Country, especially Devon, south Wales, south west Scotland and in Ireland on both sides of the border. They have a distinctive, diverse vegetation with the purple moor grass and rushes, especially the sharp-flowered rush, dominating. Orchids and rare butterflies are associated with them and so are three birds; curlew, snipe and barn owl.

They key causes of the pastures' decline are the typical agricultural improvements - increased drainage, fertiliser use and conversion to crop fields - along with over-grazing. Also to blame are land abandonment, which leads to scrub encroachment, and growing trees on these grasslands for timber. About one tenth of what remains is now covered by a range of subsidy schemes which reward farmers for wildlife-friendly farming. The action plan

■ Culm grasslands in Devon   Photography: ©P. Wakely/English Nature

calls for this to be expanded to at least 135 square kms - covering almost a quarter of what remains today - by 2000, and for five square kms of this habitat to be re-created by 2005. The cost is put at between £300,000 and £330,000 a year in 2000.

Native Pine Woodland

A large part of Scotland's uplands - 15,000 square kilometres - was once covered by a great forest dominated by Scots pine. Today only one per cent of this remains, scattered among 77 woods. In its natural state this forest, which grows on infertile, acidic soil and is fairly open, also contains birch, alder, rowan and willow trees and, down at ground level, bell heather, blueberry and crowberry. Several fairly rare insect and bird species live in these woodlands, including the capercaille. Until recently one of the big threats to the remaining forest was the planting of

fast growing timber trees like the Sitka spruce, but today the main danger comes from overgrazing by red deer and sheep which stops young trees from growing. Thus many of the remnant woodlands contain only elderly, tall trees; for decades there has been no regeneration.

But the corner may already have been turned, for new forest is now being planted or allowed to regenerate naturally and much of what remains is conserved A large proportion of the total area of Scots pine woodlands is owned by conservation organisations like the Royal Society for the Protection of Birds, or the Government's Forestry Commission. This has signed up to saving the Scots pine and the grants it pays to landowners now favour regeneration, new planting and elimination of the overgrazing which has done so much damage. The commission also has a register of seed collection areas to try to conserve the genetic diversity of the slightly different kinds of Scots pine found across the country. The action plan for this habitat proposes that, by 2005, a third of the remnants should be managed so that they regenerate and expand. By that year new pinewoods

fowl like the widgeon and a sheltered home for a variety of invertebrates, algae, baby flatfish and young squid and cuttlefish.

■ Scots Pine Canopy

Photography: Hugh Clark/WWF

should also be established over a total of 250 square kilometres through tree planting or natural self-seeding. The costs would run to £350,000 a year in 2000.

Seagrass Beds

Sea grasses are one of a tiny handful of flowering plants - or higher plants - which can live under the sea (seaweeds are all algae, a simpler form of plant). The three closely related species of sea grass found in Britain, so called because their slender, straight leaves look like grass, form underwater meadows in very shallow, sheltered areas with sandy or muddy bottoms and in the intertidal zone between the low and high tide marks. They cannot grow where there are strong waves. Sea grasses provide food for water-

The beds are found in inlets and estuaries, but they only cover a few dozen square kilometres off Britain with the largest known areas in the Cromarty Firth near Inverness and Maplin Sands off Southend. The sea grasses seem to be fairly fragile, with large diebacks occasionally being caused by disease, overgrazing by wildfowl, severe storms, very low tides and high temperatures. Pollution and over-enrichment by artificial fertilisers washing down rivers into the sea may also be doing them harm. Dredging, land reclamation and shallow water trawling gear have all done localised damage. The action plan for this habitat calls for the range and size of Britain's sea grass beds to be maintained and the feasibility of restoring degraded areas to be assessed. The cost of restoring 10 square kilometres is put at £5 million in total.

Mesotrophic Lakes

These lakes are quite rare in Britain, and found mostly on the edge of uplands in the north and west. What singles them out is their water's narrow range of concentrations of nitrate and phosphate - dissolved mineral fertilisers used by plants. Mesotrophic lakes have concentrations in the middle of the range. They support a greater variety of larger, visible water plants (as opposed to the microscopic algae) than any other kind of lake or pond and they also have a broad variety of water insects and rare fish such as the vendace. They are threatened by receiving too much nutrient, a process known as eutrophication. In eutrophic lakes the microscopic algae grow explosively in spring and summer, outcompeting the larger water plants and turning the water murky green. Lough Neagh, the great lake in the middle of Northern Ireland, was once mesotrophic but it is now no longer in this category.

Fertiliser running off farmland and cattle slurry spillages have harmed these lakes, as has effluent from sewage works and fish farms. If too much water is taken from the streams draining into them that raises the nutrient concentration too. The ploughing up of grasslands to grow crops washes silt from the land into the lakes, bringing nutrients with it and preventing life-giving sunlight from penetrating the muddied waters and reaching the aquatic plants on the lake bottom in spring. The introduction of fish species which root in the lake-floor mud, stirring up sediment and releasing nutrients, has also helped damage this scarce and declining habitat. The action plan calls for those lakes which are still mesotrophic to be maintained and for effective work to start on remediating the polluted ones by 2010. The measures will cost an estimated £350,000 a year.

Appendix Three

ORGANISATIONS TO CONTACT

Below are most of the organisations working in the field of nature and landscape conservation and biodiversity in Britain.

Leading environmental/ conservation charities and pressure groups

Council for the Protection of Rural England, Warwick House,25 Buckingham Palace Road, London SW1W 0PP. Tel: 0171 976 6433.

Friends of the Earth, 26-28 Underwood Street, London N1 7JQ. Tel: 0171 490 1555. (They will have numbers and addresses for their Welsh and Scottish offices).

Greenpeace UK, Canonbury Villas, London N1 2PN. Tel: 0171 865 8100.

National Trust, 36 Queen Anne's Gate, London SW1H 9AS. Tel: 0171 222 9251.

National Trust for Scotland, 5 Charlotte Square, Edinburgh EH2 4DU Scotland. Tel: 0131 226 5922.

Royal Society for the Protection of Birds, The Lodge, Sandy, Bedfordshire SG19 2DL. Tel: 01767 680551.

Scottish Wildlife Trust, Cramond House, Kirk Crammond, Cramond Glebe Road, Edinburgh, EH4 6NS. Tel: 0131 312 7765.

Ulster Wildlife Trust, 3 New Line, Killyleagh Road, Crossgar, Co Down, BT30 9EP. Tel: 01396 830282.

The Wildlife Trusts, The Green, Witham Park, Waterside South, Lincoln LN5 7JR.

Tel: 01522 544400. A national network of 47 local and regional trusts which conserve wildlife in town and country and look after more than 2,000 nature reserves.

World Wide Fund for Nature UK, Panda House, Weyside Park, Godalming, Surrey GU4 8JX. Tel: 01483 426444.

World Wide Fund for Nature, Scotland, 1 Crieff Road, Aberfeldy, Perthshire PH15 2BJ.

Government departments

Department of the Environment, 2 Marsham Street, London SW1P 3EB. Tel: 0171 276 3000.

Department of the Environment (Northern Ireland), Parliament Buildings, Stormont, Belfast, BT4 3SS. Tel: 01232 763210.

Ministry of Agriculture, Fisheries and Food, 3 Whitehall Place, London SW1A 2HH. Tel: 0171 270 3000.

Scottish Office, St Andrew's House, Edinburgh EH1 3TG. Tel: 0131 244 1111.

Welsh Office, Information Division, Cathays Park, Cardiff CF1 3NQ. Tel: 01222 825111.

Government nature conservation bodies

English Nature, Northminster House, Peterborough PE1 1UA. Tel: 01733 340345.

Countryside Council for Wales, Helen

Roberts, Public Relations Officer, Plas Penrhos, Ffordd Penrhos, Bangor, Gwynedd LL57 2LQ. Tel: 01248 370444.

Scottish Natural Heritage, 12 Hope Terrace, Edinburgh EH9 2AS. Tel: 0131 447 4784.

Joint Nature Conservation Committee, Lizzie Wright, Monkstone House, City Road, Peterborough PE1 1YJ. Tel: 01733 62626.

Government research organisations and other government bodies.

Countryside Commission, John Dower House, Crescent Place, Cheltenham, Gloucestershire GL50 3RA. Tel: 01242 521381.

Forestry Commission, 231 Corstophine Road, Edinburgh EH12 7AT, Scotland. Tel: 0131 334 0303.

Institute of Freshwater Ecology, Windermere Laboratory, Far Sawrey, Ambleside, Cumbria LA22 0LP. Tel: 015394 42468.

Institute of Terrestrial Ecology, Monks Wood Experimental Station, Abbots Ripton, Huntingdon, Cambridgeshire PE17 2LS. Tel: 01487 773381.

Natural Environment Research Council, Polaris House, North Star Avenue, Swindon, Wilts SN2 1EU. Tel: 01793 411500.

Sea Mammal Research Unit, Gatty Marine Laboratory, University of St Andrews, St Andrews, KY16 8LB, Scotland. Tel: 01334 462630.

Other non-governmental organisations.

Bat Conservation Trust, London Ecology Centre, 45 Shelton Street, London WC2H 9HJ. Tel: 0171 240 0933.

Birdlife International, a world-wide partnership of bird bird conservation bodies. Wellbrook Court, Girton Road, Cambridge, CB3 0NA. Tel: 01223 277318.

Botanical Society of the British Isles. An association of amateur and professional botanists which organises conferences and field meetings and publishes reports and atlases. Hon Sec Mrs Mary Briggs, c/o Department of Botany, Natural History Museum Cromwell Road, London SW7 5BD. Tel: 0171 589 6323 x 8701.

British Association of Nature Conservationists, Lings House, Billing Lings, Northamtpon NN3 8BE. Tel: 01604 405285.

British Bryological Society. Promotes the study of liverworts and mosses. Dr M.E.Newton, Honorary General Secretary, Botany Department, Liverpool Museum, William Brown Street, Liverpool L3 8EN.

British Dragonfly Society, Dr W.H.Wain, Honorary Secretary, The Hawain, Hollywater Road, Bordon, Hampshire GU35 0AD. Tel: 01420 472329.

British Entomology and Natural History Society, Hon Sec: A. Godfrey, 10 Moorlea Drive, Baildon, Shipley, W. Yorks BP17 6QL. Tel: 01274 594368

British Lichen Society, Dr O.W.Purvis, Secretary, Department of Botany, Natural History Museum, Cromwell Road, London SW7 5BD. Tel: 0171 938 8852.

British Mycological Society, studies fungi. Dr Stephen Moss, Hon Gen Sec, School of Biological Sciences, University of Portsmouth, King Henry Building,

Portsmouth, Hants PO1 2DY. Tel: 01705 525902/876543.

British Phycological Society, promotes the study of algae including seaweeds. Dr E.J.Cox, Hon Sec, Department of Botany, Natural History Museum, Cromwell Road, London SW7 5BD. Tel: 0171 938 9001.

British Pteridological Society, promotes the study and conservation of ferns. A.R.Busby, Hon Sec, c/o Natural History Museum, Cromwell Road, London SW7 5BD. Tel: 01203 715690.

British Trust for Conservation Volunteers, organises practical conservation work by tens of thousands of volunteers each year. Emily Mason, Information Officer, 36 St Mary's Street, Wallingford, Oxfordshire OX10 OEU. Tel: 01491 839766.

British Trust for Ornithology, promotes research by amateur and professional ornithologits into UK birds. The Nunnery, Nunnery Place, Thetford, Norfolk IP24 2PU. Tel: 01842 750050.

Butterfly Conservation, Deborah Scullion, Office Manager, PO Box 222, Dedham, Colchester, Essex CO7 6EY. Tel: 01206 322342.

Conchological Society. (Promotes study of land and water snails). Dr Martin Willing, Conservation Officer, 14 Goodwood Close, Midhurst, West Sussex. GU29 9JG Tel:.

Council for National Parks, a charity which campaigns to keep Britain's national parks beautiful and unspoilt. Amanda Nobbs, Director, 246 Lavender Hill, London SW11 1LJ. Tel: 0171 924 4077.

Council for the Protection of Rural Wales, Ty Gwyn, 31 High Street, Welshpool,

Powys SY21 7JP, Wales. Tel: 01938 552525/556212.

The Environment Council, a charity with a particular interest in solving environmental conflicts and informing managers and firms about the business opportunities in reducing waste and pollution. Publishes 'Who's who in the environment' £12.50. 21 Elizabeth Street, London SW1W 9RP. Tel: 0171 824 8411.

Environmental Information Service assists enquirers to find organisations and individuals involved with the environment. PO Box 197, Cawston, Norwich, Norfolk NR10 4BH. Tel: 01603 871048.

Farming and Wildlife Advisory Group, aims to help landowners combine farming and forestry with wildlife and landscape conservation. National Agricultural Centre, Stoneleigh, Kenilworth, Warwickshire CV8 2RX. Tel: 01203 696699.

Fauna and Flora International, founded in 1903, promotes conservation projects, monitoring and research overseas. Great Eastern House, Tenison Road,Cambridge CB1 2DT. Tel: 01233 461471

Game Conservancy Trust, a charity which funds and pursues research into conserving game mammals and brids in their natural habitat. Burgate Manor, Fordingbridge, Hampshire, Hants SP6 1EF. Tel: 01425 652381.

Herpetological Conservation Trust, a charity which conserves threatened amphibians and reptiles in their natural habitat. 655A Christchurch Road, Boscombe, Bournemouth BH1 4AP. Tel: 01202 391319

Mammal Society, 15 Cloisters Business Centre, 8 Battersea Park Road, London SW8 4BG. Tel: 0171 498 4358.

Marine Conservation Society, 9 Gloucester Road, Ross-on-Wye, Herefordshire HR9 5BU. Tel: 01989 566017.

The Natural History Museum, Cromwell Road, London SW7 5BD. Tel: 0171 938 9123.

Plantlife, a leading plant conservation charity. Dr Jane Smart, director, c/o Natural History Museum, Cromwell Road, London SW7 5BD. Tel: 0171 938 9111.

Royal Botanic Gardens, Christine Brandt, Head of Public Relations, Kew, Richmond, Surrey TW9 3AB. Tel: 0181 940 1171.

Royal Botanic Gardens, Edinburgh, 20a Inverleigh Row, Edinburgh, EH3 5LR. 0131 552 7171.

Vincent Wildlife Trust, funds conservation-related research on mammals. T.J. O'Connor, Secretary, 10 Lovat Lane, London EC3R 8DC. Tel: 0171 283 2089.

Wildfowl and Wetlands Trust, Slimbridge, Gloucestershire GL2 7BT. 01453 890333.

World Conservation Monitoring Centre, Jo Taylor, Information Officer, 219c Huntingdon Road, Cambridge CB3 0DL. Tel: 01223 277314.

Zoological Society of London (London and Whipsnade zoos), Regent's Park, London NW1 4RY. Tel: 0171 722 3333.